The aim of the **Overcoming** series is to enable people with psychologically based disorders to take control of their own recovery program. Each title, with its specially tailored program, is devised by a practicing clinician using the latest techniques of cognitive behavioral therapy – techniques which have been shown to be highly effective in changing the way patients think about themselves and their problems.

The series was initiated in 1993 by Peter Cooper, Professor of Psychology at Reading University and Research Fellow at the University of Cambridge, whose original volume on overcoming bulimia nervosa and binge-eating continues to help many people in the USA, the UK and Europe.

Other titles in the series include:

OVERCOMING PANIC AND AGORAPHOBIA

*A self-help guide using
Cognitive Behavioral Techniques*

DERRICK SILOVE

AND

VIJAYA MANICAVASAGAR

BASIC
BOOKS

A member of the Perseus Books Group
New York

Published by Basic Books,
A Member of the Perseus Books Group
All rights reserved. Printed in Great Britain.
No part of this book may be reproduced in any matter
whatsoever without written permission expect in the case of brief
quotations embodied in critical articles and reviews.
For information, address
Basic Books, 387 Park Avenue South,
New York, NY 10016 8810

Books published by Basic Books are available at special discounts
for bulk purchases in the United States by corporations, institutions
and other organizations. For more information, please contact
the Special Markets Department at the Perseus Books Group,
2300 Chestnut Street, Suite 200, Philadelphia, PA 19103,
or call (800) 255-1514, or e-mail special.markets@perseusbooks.com

First published in the UK in 1997 by Constable & Robinson Ltd.

A CIP catalog record for this book is available from the Library of Congress.

ISBN 978-0-465-01107-0

Important Note
This books is not intended as a substitute for medical advice or treatment.
Any person with a condition requiring medical attention should consult a
qualified medical practitioner or suitable therapist.

10 9 8 7 6 5 4 3 2 1

Table of contents

Introduction by Professor Peter Cooper

Why a cognitive behavioral approach?

Over the past two or three decades, there has been something of a revolution in the field of psychological treatment. Freud and his followers had a major impact on the way in which psychological therapy was conceptualized, and psychoanalysis and psychodynamic psychotherapy dominated the field for the first half of this century. So, long-term treatments were offered which were designed to uncover the childhood roots of personal problems – offered, that is, to those who could afford it. There was some attempt by a few health service practitioners with a public conscience to modify this form of treatment (by, for example, offering short-term treatment or group therapy), but the demand for help was so great that this had little impact. Also, whilst numerous case histories can be found of people who are convinced that psychotherapy did help them, practitioners of this form of therapy showed remarkably little interest in demonstrating that what they were offering their patients was, in fact, helpful.

As a reaction to the exclusivity of psychodynamic therapies and the slender evidence for its usefulness, in the 1950s and 1960s a set of techniques was developed, broadly collectively termed 'behavior therapy'. These techniques shared two basic features. First, they aimed to remove symptoms (such as anxiety) by dealing with those symptoms themselves, rather than their deep-seated underlying historical causes. Second, they were techniques, loosely related to what laboratory psychologists were finding out about the mechanisms of learning, which were formulated in testable terms. Indeed, practitioners of behavior therapy were committed to using techniques of proven value or, at worst, of a form which could potentially be put to test. The area where these techniques proved of most value was in the treatment of anxiety disorders, especially specific phobias (such as fear of animals or heights) and agoraphobia, both notoriously difficult to treat using conventional psychotherapies.

After an initial flush of enthusiasm, discontent with behavior therapy grew. There were a number of reasons for this, an important one of which was the fact that behavior therapy did not deal with the internal thoughts which were so obviously central to the distress that patients were experiencing. In this context, the fact that behavior therapy proved so inadequate when it came to the treatment of depression highlighted the need for major revision. In the late 1960s and early 1970s a treatment was developed specifically for depression called 'cognitive therapy'. The pioneer in this enterprise was an American psychiatrist, Professor Aaron T. Beck, who developed a theory of depression which emphasized the importance of people's depressed styles of thinking. He also specified a new form of therapy. It would not be an exaggeration to say that Beck's work has changed the nature of psychotherapy, not just for depression but for a range of psychological problems.

In recent years the cognitive techniques introduced by Beck have been merged with the techniques developed earlier by the behavior therapists to produce a body of theory and practice which has come to be known as 'cognitive behavior therapy'. There are two main reasons why this form of treatment has come to be so important within the field of psychotherapy. First, cognitive therapy for depression, as originally described by Beck and developed by his successors, has been subjected to the strictest scientific testing; and it has been found to be a highly successful treatment for a significant proportion of cases of depression. Not only has it proved to be as effective as the best alternative treatments (except in the most severe cases, where medication is required), but some studies suggest that people treated successfully with cognitive behavior therapy are less likely to experience a later recurrence of their depression than people treated successfully with other forms of therapy (such as antidepressant medication). Second, it has become clear that specific patterns of thinking are associated with a range of psychological problems and that treatments which deal with these styles of thinking are highly effective. So, specific cognitive behavioral treatments have been developed for anxiety disorders, like panic disorder, generalized anxiety disorder, specific phobias and social phobia, obsessive compulsive disorders, and hypochondriasis (health anxiety), as well as for other conditions such as compulsive gambling, alcohol and drug addiction, and eating disorders like bulimia nervosa and binge-eating disorder. Indeed, cognitive behavioral techniques have a wide application beyond the narrow categories of psychological disorders: they have been applied effectively, for example, to helping people with low self-esteem and those with marital difficulties.

At any one time almost 10 per cent of the general population is suffering from depression, and more than 10 per cent has one or other of the anxiety disorders. Many others have a range of psychological problems and personal difficulties. It is of the greatest importance that treatments of proven effectiveness are developed. However, even when the armoury of therapies is, as it were, full, there remains a very great problem – namely that the delivery of treatment is expensive and the resources are not going to be available evermore. Whilst this shortfall could be met by lots of people helping themselves, commonly the natural inclination to make oneself feel better in the present is to do precisely those things which perpetuate or even exacerbate one's problems. For example, the person with agoraphobia will stay at home to prevent the possibility of an anxiety attack; and the person with bulimia nervosa will avoid eating all potentially fattening foods. Whilst such strategies might resolve some immediate crisis, they leave the underlying problem intact and provide no real help in dealing with future difficulties.

So, there is a twin problem here; although effective treatments have been developed, they are not widely available; and when people try to help themselves they often make matters worse. In recent years the community of cognitive behavior therapists have responded to this situation. What they have done is to take the principles and techniques of specific cognitive behavior therapies for particular problems and represent them in self-help manuals. These manuals specify a systematic program of treatment which the individual sufferer is advised to work through to overcome their difficulties. In this way, the cognitive behavioral therapeutic techniques of proven value are being made available on the widest possible basis.

Self-help manuals are never going to replace therapists. Many people will need individual treatment from a qualified therapist. It is also the case that, despite the widespread success of cognitive behavioral therapy, some people will not respond to it and will need one of the other treatments available. Nevertheless, although research on the use of cognitive behavioral self-help manuals is at an early stage, the work done to date indicates that for a very great many people such a manual will prove sufficient for them to overcome their problems without professional help.

Many people suffer silently and secretly for years. Sometimes appropriate help is not forthcoming despite their efforts to find it. Sometimes they feel too ashamed or guilty to reveal their problems to anyone. For many of these people the cognitive behavioral self-help manual will provide a lifeline to recovery and a better future.

Professor Peter Cooper
The University of Reading, 1997

PART ONE

About Panic Attacks and Agoraphobia

Prologue

'A day in my life'

As I approach the bus, the symptoms become much worse. It's like being hit by a tornado. My mouth goes dry, my heart starts pounding, I feel sick in my stomach, I can hardly breathe, and my hands are shaking. I am sure that I am going to faint. I don't know how I manage to reach my seat – I feel as if I am just a spectator, everything seems a bit unreal and distant. Am I going crazy? I bet the other people on the bus have noticed. I really can't control my breathing any more, I feel like I am going to suffocate and die. When will it end?

By the time I get off the bus, the symptoms have lessened. Why do these attacks start and stop for no reason? I feel drained, exhausted and weak. I can't think straight. Maybe I should give up taking the bus for a while. Or should I go to the hospital for another check-up? I don't know. I can't cope with this any more. All I know is that I spend most of my time worrying about having another attack. I can't go on like this or my whole life will be ruined.

That night I lie in bed tossing and turning, and the next morning I awake exhausted. It seems ridiculous, but my mind keeps wandering back to those dreadful feelings I had on the bus. What if I have an attack when I'm out shopping? Will I be able to escape before it gets so bad that I can't reach home? I keep checking my body for symptoms. I think about those strange tingling and numb feelings I had in my hands and feet. I have heard that you can have funny feelings down your arms when you are having a heart attack. Perhaps that's what is wrong with me.

At last, I drag myself out of bed. I have that hollow feeling in the pit of my stomach and I feel a bit light-headed. I know the doctor said 'everything is OK,' but it is hard to believe that. There must be something seriously wrong with me. Maybe I should insist on seeing a specialist. They must have more accurate tests to pick up something wrong with your brain or your heart.

I am irritable with the kids at breakfast. They seem bewildered about my moodiness, but I can't tell them about my worries. What if I am seriously ill? It's better to keep it from them until I am sure. Anyway, they will just say the usual things about my worrying too much. I have an extra few cups of coffee to wake me up so that I can cope with the day. We talk about visiting mother in hospital and that seems to upset me even more. She has always been so healthy and now she has suddenly been taken ill. Life seems so unpredictable.

After seeing the kids off to school I rush to get the bus. I notice that the 'clamping' sensation is starting in my chest. I am having difficulty breathing and I feel hot and sweaty. I just hope that I don't have that 'spaced out' feeling on the bus. Why do I keep feeling like this? It seems to be getting worse. Why can't I be confident and in control the way I used to be? I must pull myself together.

1

What are panic disorder and agoraphobia?

Almost everyone feels anxious at some time in their lives. It is common to become anxious in situations such as a job interview, an examination or a public speaking engagement. Mild anxiety is so common that it is regarded as normal, and it is not usually a cause for concern. In fact, a degree of anxiety is necessary to help us perform well in situations requiring concentration, efficiency and skill. For some people, however, anxiety symptoms are so severe and persistent that they become disabling. People with such intense anxiety often are suffering from an anxiety disorder.

Many people suffer from anxiety disorders, yet only a small percentage of them seek treatment. The majority either cope on their own, suffer in silence or use risky methods (e.g. alcohol or drugs) to damp down their symptoms.

In some cases, people develop episodes of sudden and intense anxiety, known as *panic attacks*. They may not realize that they are suffering from an anxiety disorder, but instead believe that they have developed some other illness, like heart disease or stroke – which is understandable, because many of the symptoms of panic are physical. The experience of panic attacks often leads people to avoid situations where they fear experiencing further attacks.

> *I began having panic attacks when I was about nineteen, during a stressful time at work. I would become breathless and sweaty, my heart would pound, and I had pains in my chest. I became so frightened that I thought I would have a heart attack or die. After that, attacks came out of the blue, and I noticed that I was avoiding certain situations, such as visiting department stores or travelling on buses. I felt that I couldn't talk to anyone about the problem since they would think I was going crazy.*
>
> John

What is a panic attack?

> *It starts when I suddenly feel like I can't breathe properly. I then start feeling dizzy and sweaty and notice that my heart is racing. Sometimes I become nauseous or feel like I am going to choke. My fingers go numb and I have a tingling sensation in my feet. I feel strange, as if I am not really 'there', as if I am detached from reality. I start thinking that I am about to lose control or die. This makes me feel extremely frightened ... Even though the attack only lasts for five or ten minutes, it feels like forever and that I will never get over it.*
>
> Christine

A panic attack refers to a sudden burst of acute anxiety, usually accompanied by a number of physical symptoms and catastrophic thoughts. It usually lasts for between two and thirty minutes – but at the time it feels as if it will last for ever, and when it does pass it leaves the sufferer weak and exhausted. Without treatment, panic attacks can occur several times a week or even daily.

The experience of having a panic attack

Every episode is slightly different. At first I used to feel that I was about to vomit or have diarrhea. More recently, I have had this severe choking feeling and sharp pain in my chest. I realize now that those feelings of being detached from myself and the environment are part of the same pattern.

Fay

Panic attacks are particularly frightening because they appear out of the blue, or in situations in which most people do not expect to be nervous or frightened. The speed at which the symptoms occur, their intensity and the fact that they involve so many parts of the body all add to the sense of fear and helplessness. Commonly occurring symptoms include:

- difficulty breathing, or being short of breath;
- a feeling of choking;
- tightness, pressure or pain in the chest;
- shakiness, trembling and weakness;
- sweaty palms and excessive perspiration;
- tingling or numbness in the hands and feet;

- palpitations or a pounding or rapid heartbeat;
- feeling faint, dizzy or unsteady;
- feeling 'out of touch' with your body or your immediate surroundings;
- nausea, chuming or upset in the stomach or lower bowel;
- feeling hot and cold, or flushed.

Together with these physical symptoms of panic, people commonly experience distressing thoughts, such as:

- 'I'm going crazy/insane';
- 'I'm going to lose control';
- 'I'm going to faint';
- 'I'm going to collapse';
- 'I'm having a heart attack';
- 'I'm having a stroke';
- 'I'm going to start screaming and make a fool of myself.

The likelihood of any of these things happening is remote, and when the episode has ended these thoughts often seem silly or irrational; but at the time of the panic attack they can be very strong. Indeed, the fears can be so real during a panic attack that they persist at the back of the mind and lead to more worry and anxiety in between attacks.

How do people feel after a panic attack?

After a panic attack subsides, sufferers often feel exhausted, dispirited and confused. It is an intensely frightening experience, especially when you do not know what is causing it. Many people understandably believe that they are physically unwell and seek medical attention at a hospital or from their local doctor. Others feel ashamed or embarrassed by what they consider to be a lack of self-control, and suffer in silence rather than reveal their problems to others or seek professional help.

What is panic disorder?

Some people have panic attacks repeatedly and the problem begins to interfere with their lives. These people suffer from *panic disorder*. Studies report that approximately 2–4 per cent of us will experience panic disorder at some time during our lives.

Sometimes, people may suffer from just one or two severe panic attacks, and then begin to fear having another attack. Their preoccupation with the problem dominates their minds and their behavior, making them ever more anxious and perhaps causing them to adjust their lifestyles: for example, they may avoid going out for fear of having another panic attack. Such people also suffer from panic disorder, even though they do not experience frequent panic attacks.

Avoiding situations where panic attacks might occur can affect people's lives as much as actually having regular attacks. The experience of worrying that a panic attack will recur is known as *anticipatory anxiety*. Overcoming anticipatory anxiety is one of the key elements in recovery from panic disorder and agoraphobia.

What is agoraphobia?

After a while I became afraid of going shopping in case I couldn't get back home quickly enough. I felt more and more anxious waiting at the check-out, and on one occasion I had to leave my shopping trolley there and hurry home. After that, I could only go to the shops if someone came with me. My fears extended to other situations so that I began to avoid public transport and even driving in the car. Now I can hardly leave the house.

Mavis

People who have had a panic attack in a particular situation may start to find that they avoid that place for fear of having another attack. Someone who has experienced a panic attack in a large department store may begin to avoid going shopping altogether. Using public transport, entering crowded places or being in traffic may remind a person that they have had panic attacks in those situations, so that avoiding those places becomes a way of preventing further anxiety. This kind of behavior is known as *agoraphobia* – literally, translated from the Greek, 'a fear of the market place'. In reality, agoraphobic fears are more extensive than simply a fear of shopping or public places. For some people, being alone at home for any reason is enough to make them very anxious. Agoraphobia is fairly common – over 7 per cent of women and nearly 3 per cent of men suffer from the disorder at some time in their lives.

A person suffering from agoraphobia tends to avoid situations in which escape might be difficult if they have a panic attack, or else tolerates being in that situation only with great dread or apprehension. Sometimes people with agoraphobia find that they only can cope with a feared situation, such as sitting in a car in traffic or going through a tunnel, if they are accompanied by a trusted companion. Others, if they go to see a movie or play, may choose to sit in the aisle seat of the auditorium, as close to the exit as possible, so that they can 'escape' if they become anxious.

Often, these fears extend to include all situations similar to the one in which a panic attack occurred: for example, a panic attack in a restaurant may lead to avoiding all restaurants. In this way avoidance behavior can escalate, restricting people in their movements and activities, even to the point where they may become housebound.

The relationship between panic disorder and agoraphobia is complex. Quite a lot of people with panic disorder develop agoraphobia; but many do not, and they are referred to as suffering from 'pure' panic disorder. Also, agoraphobia can develop on its own or as part of another disorder, such as depression. Agoraphobia also can persist after panic attacks have subsided. If a person who is worried about having a panic attack avoids all feared situations, they may thus prevent any further panic attacks; but the avoidance can continue and become an established way of life.

Examples of situations that people with agoraphobia commonly avoid, or in which they experience anxiety, are:

- driving a car in heavy traffic;
- travelling over bridges or through tunnels;
- visiting the supermarket;
- entering a crowded shopping area;
- taking public transport;
- going out to dinner/parties, shows or movies;
- waiting in line, for example, in a hairdresser's, or in a doctor's surgery;
- being alone at home.

Why do some people develop agoraphobia?

It is not clear why some people with panic disorder develop agoraphobia. Two mechanisms may, however, contribute. First, if you have panic attacks repeatedly in a particular situation, it is natural that you will develop a fear that the anxiety will return if you approach that or a similar situation. In other words, your past experience warns you against approaching places or situations where you have experienced panic. Thus you come to experience a 'fear of fear'. Secondly, other, more automatic 'conditioning' mechanisms may be operating. We have all heard of Pavlov's dog who was conditioned to salivate every time a bell was rung. In the same way, humans can be 'conditioned' automatically to react in an anxious way to otherwise harmless situations if they repeatedly experience anxiety when they approach those places. Thus, without being aware of it, we can come to associate panic with situations where it has occurred in the past, even if those places are not genuinely dangerous. Some people may 'condition' more easily than others. They may need to experience only a few panic attacks in a department store to 'learn' to avoid that place.

The different ways individuals cope with their worries also may influence the likelihood of developing agoraphobia. Assertive persons are more likely to confront their fears, while those who tend to avoid stress tend to withdraw. People with strong fears about separation ('separation anxiety') may tend to cling to others for security, or only to go out in the company of a trusted companion. More women than men with panic disorder develop agoraphobia. One possible explanation for this is that cultural expectations encourage men and women to respond in different ways to severe anxiety. Men are expected (and therefore expect themselves) to 'soldier on' and to fight anxiety (often with the 'help' of alcohol), whereas it may be more acceptable for women to avoid situations that cause fear.

What brings on panic attacks and agoraphobia?

Many people are able to recall several stressful incidents that occurred just before they experienced panic attacks, and some of these 'stressors' may continue or worsen after the attacks have begun. Arguments with a spouse or partner, death of a family member, personal illness or problems at work are commonly reported in the weeks or months before the onset of panic attacks. Stressful life circumstances befall almost everybody and those events do not, on their own, lead to the development of panic attacks. Usually it is a combination of factors, such as being vulnerable physically and/or psychologically together with life stress, that triggers panic attacks. Stress may play a role in causing panic attacks to continue; however, as we shall see in Chapter 3, there are other factors that may cause a vicious cycle of panic to persist.

2

How do panic disorder and agoraphobia affect people's lives?

My life revolves around the fear of having another panic attack. I can't concentrate on my work, which has suffered greatly. My problem has caused family rows. My family think that I should just pull myself together and stop worrying. I have lost my self-confidence and self-respect. I don't like to socialize any more In case I embarrass myself or I am forced to leave in a hurry because of a panic attack.

Patricia

Panic attacks and agoraphobia can have a serious impact on sufferers' lives. Severe anxiety and avoidance interfere with work, studies, family relationships and social life. The constant fear of having another panic attack produces feelings of apprehension, tension and fear, making sufferers overly cautious, unadventurous and constrained in their lifestyles. It is no wonder that people with panic disorder and agoraphobia often become depressed.

Symptoms of depression

Sometimes I would start to cry and cry . . . I felt so hope-less and useless. Other people around me seemed to be able to run their own lives . . . but for me panic attacks were controlling my life. Why couldn't I just snap out of it and be OK? I started feeling more and more depressed and self-critical as I realized that I could not control the panic attacks. I lost my self-confidence, I stopped wanting to socialize, and my friends seemed to withdraw from me. Life became so difficult that the thought crossed my mind that it was not worth going on.

Geoffrey

Some sufferers of panic attacks experience periods of depression in addition to their anxiety symptoms. Between 30 per cent and 70 per cent of people with panic disorder develop depression at some time. Depression may last for hours or days at a time; for some people it may persist for weeks or even months. It may be fairly mild, for example feeling rather sad and tearful at times, or more severe, leading to feelings of hopelessness, worthlessness and failure. The depressed person may no longer feel like working or socializing – not only from the fear of having a panic attack, but also because of the low self-esteem, loss of interest and lack of enjoyment that accompany severe demoralization.

Feelings of depression can be made worse by the sense of shame that accompanies uncontrollable anxiety. Shame makes people secretive about their anxiety, so that they make excuses to avoid social situations rather than having to suffer the embarrassment of revealing their problem to their friends. This may lead to a vicious cycle of avoiding enjoyable activities (like seeing a movie with friends, or going out for dinner), thus increasing feelings of isolation which worsen depression and lead to further loss of motivation. The person may begin to feel helpless and hopeless and then become more self-critical and withdrawn. People with agoraphobia are likely to become depressed because of their greatly restricted activities. In this way symptoms of anxiety, avoidance and depression interact to cause greater suffering and disability. It is important to recognize these vicious cycles and to attempt to break them in the process of recovery.

People suffering from panic attacks may feel quite desperate at times. It may seem impossible to improve their situation. They may begin to overeat, to use alcohol excessively or to take drugs in the attempt to forget about their problems or blot out their symptoms. When panic symptoms are complicated by severe depression or other problems, there is a risk of serious self-harm, even suicide. Clearly, it is important to take steps towards recovery long before such a level of desperation is reached.

For most sufferers of panic disorder and agoraphobia, depression lifts when anxiety symptoms are brought under control. In those few instances where depression lingers after the anxiety has improved, it is important to seek specific professional help. Some people suffer a mixture of anxiety and depressive symptoms; in others, depression is the main problem, with anxiety symptoms being secondary. If you are in doubt as to which is the main problem – anxiety or depression – you should consult your doctor or the local mental health service.

Effects on social life

My anxiety problem has taken over my whole life. Even though I have a close family, I can't talk to any of them about it since they don't understand what I am going through. My problem has created a wall between me and my husband. Also, I become terribly embarrassed with my friends when I start developing panic symp-toms. I can't face seeing people.

Joanne

Panic attacks can have a profound effect on family and social life. Often, the situations in which panic attacks occur are those that involve being out of the house among other people. It is understandable that a person who experiences panic attacks at a movie or in a restaurant will be apprehensive about returning to such places and may even avoid them. Sufferers may make excuses not to go on social outings, especially if it means entering situations in which they fear they might panic. Friends and family may become frustrated and offended when their invitations are regularly turned down. On the other hand, some panic sufferers who have disclosed their symptoms to those close to them find that their problems are not taken seriously and that they are given superficial advice, for example 'pull yourself together' or 'be strong'. These responses may seem insensitive, but it must be remembered that most non-sufferers have very little knowledge about panic attacks and agoraphobia, and they may not understand how difficult it can be to overcome these problems. It is common for people to believe that because it is common to experience anxiety, everyone should be able to cope with it by using will-power.

Severe anxiety can disturb intimate relationships. Anxiety can cause a sufferer to be irritable, preoccupied, withdrawn or in need of repeated reassurance. Sufferers may come to depend heavily on their spouses or partners to carry out everyday chores such as shopping, banking or collecting the children from school. A sufferer may feel that the problem is not understood by a spouse or partner, who in turn feels baffled, frustrated and helpless. Thus a vicious circle of misunderstanding can set in.

The social and personal relationships of those who suffer from panic attacks and agoraphobia commonly are transformed when they recover from the acute symptoms and learn how to master their anxiety. They often feel much happier within their family and social networks, and their spouses or partners are greatly relieved. Occasionally, because the family's lifestyle has adapted gradually to the sufferer's restricted activities, recovery will require other family members to change their own habits and expectations. The household has to adjust to a member who is more active, assertive and independent than they are used to. Such adjustments can cause tension and uncertainty within the family. There are some advantages in having a parent or spouse who is always at home!

3

What causes panic and agoraphobia?

A number of factors act together to cause panic attacks and panic disorder. The particular combination will vary from one person to another. It is useful, however, to think of a chain of factors of broadly three types that together progressively build up to produce panic.

- First, some people are *vulnerable* as a result of the way they are built (their constitution) or because of experiences they have had in early life.
- Then there are immediate stresses or *triggers* that bring on a sudden panic attack.
- Finally, there are a number of influences (*perpetuating factors*) that keep the process going, often leading to a vicious cycle in which panic attacks are made worse or brought on more frequently.

This chapter will outline how these *vulnerability, trigger* and *perpetuating* factors are at present understood.

Vulnerability to panic attacks and agoraphobia

Are some people more vulnerable than others to developing panic attacks and agoraphobia? Certainly there seem to be physical, psychological and social factors that put some of us at greater risk. Some of these factors relate to early life, and others to adulthood.

Risk factors in early life

When I was young I was very afraid of the dark. I hated being alone and worried that I might be kidnapped. If my parents went out I kept thinking that they would be killed in an accident or attacked. These thoughts made me very insecure.

Paul

In some (but not all) instances, panic disorder runs in families. This can be a matter of genetic inheritance and/or the nature of family relationships – whether openly affectionate or cold, supportive or demanding, etc. Identical twins share similar levels of 'trait anxiety' – that is, the temperamental tendency to worry or be nervy – which suggests that, to some extent, we inherit our tendency to develop symptoms such as panic. Many adults with agoraphobia recall their family environments as being somewhat cold and unsupportive. Some children who are vulnerable to later panic disorder have high levels of 'separation anxiety' in early life which makes them clingy, insecure, afraid of being alone and sometimes unwilling to go to school. Clearly, interactions between children and their parents are always complex, and it is important not to blame one or the other for creating anxiety. It is difficult to be sure whether, for example, parental overprotectiveness causes the child to feel insecure or whether some anxious children demand more and are less satisfied with the attention they receive from their parents.

Children who are exposed to shocking events, abuse and trauma in early life appear to run an increased risk of panic disorder as they grow up. Indeed, such experiences make children vulnerable to a wide range of emotional difficulties in adulthood, of which panic disorder is just one. However, some events may be particularly significant for later panic symptoms: for example, events that cause difficulty in breathing in early life (e.g. near-drowning, suffocation, severe attacks of asthma) may sensitize the nervous system to changes in blood gas levels. If someone who has had such an experience becomes anxious, or hyperventilates, in later life, he or she may be more likely to develop full-blown panic attacks.

Factors in later life

Psychological factors

Why can't I control myself? Perhaps I should stop going out altogether. That way I can make sure that I won't have any more of these terrible attacks. I am sure that something terrible is going to happen during one of these attacks. My life seems to be completely out of control.

Walter

People who are prone to having panic attacks often think in particular ways. They are more likely to interpret bodily sensations (e.g. a racing heartbeat) in a catastrophic way, jumping to the conclusion that they are having a heart attack. Most people are able to counter unrealistic fears with more positive, reassuring thoughts ('That twinge of pain in my lower chest is probably just a bit of indigestion'). People who are prone to catastrophic interpretations, on the other hand, tend to believe that they are unable to control their lives or the world around them. They may slip quickly into thinking that problems are too great to tackle and beyond their capacity to solve. This means that they are more likely to become worried and stressed when they encounter real-life problems. A negative thinking style may grow out of a family setting in which a child was not reassured enough or encouraged to develop confidence. Or again, it may become established where a vulnerable person has suffered a major disruption in the family or other severe trauma in early life which has undermined his or her self-esteem. Events like this often seem uncontrollable at the time, leading to the feeling that life is worryingly unpredictable and that problems are impossible to solve.

Such negative thinking may affect the way you deal with stress. Different people have different ways of coping with stress or stressful situations. Some methods are more helpful than others, and some individuals cope better than others in similar situations. Coping skills are largely learnt and become a habit by repeated use. Children often learn ways of coping with stress from the people around them – parents, teachers and friends.

Some negative coping styles include:

- giving up or becoming frustrated when you face obstacles in life;
- avoiding situations that cause discomfort;
- becoming tense and irritable if you cannot get your way immediately;
- depending too much on others for help;
- taking excessive amounts of alcohol or drugs to dampen unpleasant feelings.

If you are susceptible to anxiety, negative coping styles like these can actually make the symptoms worse. Breaking old coping habits and learning new, more helpful ones can be difficult and requires a lot of practice.

Social factors

I have been working day and night for the exams and have had little time to go out with Sam. It is hard to know why things are so cold between us. Is it because I am so busy or are the attacks I am having making me more irritable? He seems confused about our relationship but I am scared to tell him about the attacks in case he thinks I am crazy or weak. At the same time, I need his support even more now that my confidence is so low.

Yvonne

People from all walks of life develop panic attacks and panic disorder. However, women are at greater risk than men. Why this should be so remains unclear. The answer may have something to do with the role of women in modern society, or with genetic or hormonal factors, or – partly, and in some cases – to the stress of childbearing and childrearing. It has been suggested that women are pulled in opposite directions in the modern world, finding it hard to be both a home-builder and also a breadwinner. Difficulties in relationships appear to be important in panic disorder – but, as we have already seen, this is a complex area. Although chronic stress within marriages and other long-term partnerships may be an important factor, many people who develop panic attacks are single. It is not always easy to be sure whether the stress within the family is a cause or a result of one member having panic disorder. For example, if a partner is 'dominant' this may be to compensate for the panic sufferer's insecurity, or it may be a factor that is increasing the sufferer's level of anxiety and dependence. It may even be both.

Physical factors

I had spasms in my chest in which I felt that I could not breathe, that my chest was in a vice, and that pins were being stuck into my heart. I kept going back to the hospital, but they said they could find "nothing wrong". The symptoms were so real, I was sure they were missing something serious like a heart attack.

Frank

People who suffer from panic attacks commonly ask whether their symptoms are real or just a result of their 'imagination'. To begin to understand panic attacks, it is important to consider the normal 'stress response'. A sudden shock or threat causes extreme fear in anyone. Think how you would react if a car suddenly turned a corner at high speed and narrowly missed you as you crossed the street; or if someone unexpectedly slammed a door behind you. You are suddenly very alert and vigilant; your skin crawls, your heart may pound, and you may become a bit shaky. You may jump up, shout or get angry. This is the normal *'fight or flight'* response which helps us to take defensive action when we feel threatened. The response is controlled by the centres of the nervous system buried deep in the brain. These centres control the involuntary (or 'automatic') nervous system, which controls the muscles of the internal organs and glands of the body. The involuntary nervous system is activated immediately when the brain receives a threatening message from the outside world. It responds instantaneously and without any conscious prompting from us. When those nerves send out an alarm signal, the muscles of the heart contract faster, leading to rapid beats or palpitations, the muscles of the chest wall contract, causing you to breathe more quickly, and the perspiration glands squeeze more sweat on to the skin. The involuntary nervous system also activates hormone glands which release chemicals such as adrenalin into the blood. Those chemicals prepare the body for rapid action by sending more blood to the muscles, by releasing sugar to give you more energy and by making you alert to the environment.

This fear reaction is essential and could save your life in an emergency. The associated physical sensations are caused by actual physiological changes, and usually pass after the threat has disappeared. However, in panic disorder, the 'fight or flight' response is activated inappropriately, when there is no direct threat present. It may be that some people have a lower 'trigger' threshold or that their control mechanism in the nervous system for bringing the fight or flight response to an end is less efficient. Temperamental factors, such as an ingrained tendency to worry, together with continuing stress over a period of time, may increase the general level of bodily tension so that you are operating closer and closer to the trigger threshold. Even minor events may then set off the fight or flight response, leading to panic. Because, as we saw above, vulnerable people interpret upsetting experiences or bodily sensations as more threatening than others, they keep sending 'false alarms' to the centre that triggers the fight or flight reaction. It is when the fight or flight response is triggered inappropriately in situations that, although stressful, are not really dangerous, that you experience the symptoms of a panic attack. The fight and flight response itself is a normal and useful mechanism aimed at protecting the body from danger. Thus, for people who are otherwise healthy, the physical symptoms of panic, although frightening, are not directly damaging to your health. This is a very important point to grasp, as one of the greatest fears that beset panic sufferers is that the attacks themselves are doing them harm.

Anxiety mechanisms in the nervous system

A lot of research has been done into what goes on in the brain immediately before and during extreme anxiety and panic attacks. It is known that certain chemicals, called 'neurotransmitters', pass messages from one nerve to another in the brain. A number of these chemicals are thought to be important in the nerves that transmit fear, alarm and anxiety 'messages'. It is still not clear how these 'messenger' systems may differ in anxiety sufferers; but it nevertheless seems that many of the medications that affect anxiety (see Chapter 4) act to alter the actions of these neurotransmitters or the way the nerve endings respond to these 'messengers'. If there are differences in the nervous system of panic sufferers, then these are of a very subtle kind and probably relate to the fine balance of certain chemicals and their actions in particular brain pathways. In other words, ordinary tests (such as X-rays or brain scans) invariably are normal in sufferers of panic disorder. If abnormalities are detected, then the person is likely to be suffering not from a primary panic disorder but from one of the relatively rare physical illnesses that sometimes can mimic panic.

Physical illnesses that can cause panic-like symptoms

Rarely, physical illness can mimic panic disorder. For example, people who have problems with their thyroid gland (which normally regulates the body's temperature and the rate at which chemicals are processed) may experience symptoms that are very like those of anxiety and panic. Usually, other accompanying symptoms will make it clear that a physical disorder is present. Occasionally, anxiety-like symptoms will be the first sign of such an underlying illness.

Some conditions that may cause panic-like symptoms include:

- irregular heart rhythms, and occasionally, disease of the heart blood vessels;
- disorders affecting your breathing;
- excessive use of certain medications, e.g. for asthma;
- rare disorders of the glands that produce hormones and other chemicals in the blood;
- unusual types of epilepsy;
- excessive use of or withdrawal from caffeine, drugs or alcohol.

If you have any concern that you may have a serious physical illness, it is important for your doctor to take a full medical history, to examine you, and to carry out some investigations such as blood tests. If there is any likelihood of heart disease, then an electrocardiogram, a 'stress test' and some blood tests can usually identify if there is an active problem. Most likely, these tests will show that you are physically healthy and you can then be quite certain that your symptoms are due to anxiety. If these tests do show some sort of physical illness (e.g. thyroid disease), it is very likely that treatment of this problem will also reduce your anxiety-like symptoms. It is possible to suffer from both a physical illness (for example, asthma or heart disease) and panic disorder, and anyone in this situation will require treatment for both conditions. In the majority of sufferers, however, no associated physical illness is found.

While it is very seldom that panic disorder is caused by physical illness, the symptoms can be so dramatic that it is difficult for the sufferer to believe that there is no physical condition underlying the problem. Consequently, he or she may visit several doctors or insist on repeating blood tests or on having more complicated investigations. The procedures themselves may cause stress and reinforce the fear that there 'must be something wrong'. It is helpful to remember that one of the common symptoms of panic disorder is an uncontrollable worry about having a physical illness. If tests performed by the doctor rule out a physical illness, then it is best to reassess the situation and to focus on managing the anxiety symptoms rather than to have unnecessary additional tests.

What sets off a panic attack?

Hyperventilation and panic symptoms

A common 'trigger' of panic symptoms in those who are susceptible to them is 'overbreathing' or 'hyperventilation'. Many people who suffer from panic attacks notice that their breathing rate increases and becomes shallow while they are in the midst of an attack. Vulnerable people may in fact be hyperventilating chronically, but this may not be obvious. Signs of hyperventilation include shallow, frequent breathing, gasping, sighing, yawning or panting. Two common signs of chronic hyperventilation are excessive sighing and yawning. Few people realize that yawning may not be caused by boredom or sighing by sadness, but that both may be signs of anxiety! If you notice that you are sighing and yawning through the day, you may be chronically overbreathing and therefore at risk of provoking panic symptoms and panic attacks. Normally, there is a balance between the gases oxygen and carbon dioxide in the blood. Hyperventilation causes more than usual amounts of carbon dioxide to be breathed out, making it difficult for the red blood cells to release oxygen to the body. In other words, the harder you breathe, the less oxygen you are delivering to the brain! Hyperventilation thus results in typical symptoms of panic such as unsteadiness, dizziness, feeling 'spaced out' and weakness. Hyperventilation increases under stress and, in chronic overbreathers, may trigger a panic attack. Once the panic attack starts, breathing then becomes more rapid, and the 'hyperventilation – panic' cycle begins. Also, catastrophic misinterpretation of the physical symptoms of hyperventilation can lead to greater anxiety and panic. Thus a vicious cycle results, as shown in Figure 1.

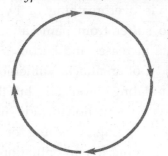

Hyperventilation/overbreathing

Increase in breathing rate

Physical symptoms (light-headedness, dizziness, tingling)

Misinterpretation

Panic symptoms/panic attacks

Figure 1. The connection between hyperventilation and panic symptoms

Misusing alcohol, drugs and medications

I found that if I had a few beers before going out, then I was less likely to have the attacks. Over time, I needed to drink more to control the attacks. I found that I woke up shaky in the morning and I needed to have a drink immediately to calm down. I then lost track whether I was still having panic attacks or just needed another drink.

Bill

One of the most important physical factors contributing to anxiety in panic sufferers is the misuse of alcohol, drugs or other stimulants. People with panic disorder may attempt to comfort themselves by smoking or drinking cups of coffee or strong tea, but in reality they are provoking their nervous systems with strong stimulants. The excessive use of these stimulants can lower the panic threshold and make it more likely that further attacks will occur. Panic attacks also can be triggered or made worse by the use of marijuana, cocaine, amphetamines and other stimulant drugs.

If you suffer from panic attacks it can be very tempting to turn to alcohol and sedative drugs (such as barbiturates) in an attempt to dampen symptoms of panic or to give you the courage to go out. But as many sufferers who have tried this 'cure' will know, the positive effect is only short-lived; excessive alcohol or drug use makes anxiety worse in the long run. As the amount of alcohol you need to control your anxiety increases, so you are more likely to experience withdrawal symptoms (such as the 'shakes') when you are not drinking. Sedative drugs can have the same effects. These withdrawal effects are very similar to symptoms of panic and therefore complicate the underlying anxiety disorder.

As with many of the other contributory factors we have discussed, the relationship between alcohol or drug use and panic disorder is complex. It is important to decide which came first, the anxiety or the alcohol. It may be clear that panic attacks or anxiety symptoms were experienced before heavy drinking began. In such cases, even though alcohol use is a secondary problem, it can cause dependence as well as damaging organs of the body (for example, the liver, stomach and brain), leading to physical illness and psychological problems including anxiety. If, on the other hand, panic symptoms are secondary to alcohol dependence, then the anxiety symptoms will improve when the drinking is brought under control. Even if the anxiety is primary, the alcohol problem may have become entrenched, and if this is the case it will need treatment in its own right, It is rarely possible to overcome panic disorder if alcohol abuse is continuing.

What keeps the vicious cycle going?

Many people have one or two panic attacks in their lives when they are under extreme stress. Although the experience is very unpleasant, it is soon forgotten and does not continue to affect their lives. For some people, though, a self-perpetuating mechanism or vicious cycle is set up which causes panic attacks to recur like a chain reaction. The factors

that may cause this reaction can be divided into psychological, social and physical factors.

Psychological factors

As we have already seen, 'fear of fear' and 'fear of illness'
can greatly increase the risk that one panic attack may
lead to another. In some ways, sufferers and their nervous
systems are tricking each other. Initially, a vulnerable
person may be under great stress, perhaps from work or
home life, so that without being aware of it, she is very
close to the tension threshold for triggering a panic attack.
A small added stress, such as noise, light, crowding and
the frustrations of going shopping, pushes her over that
threshold, and she has a panic attack. In other words, the
automatic nervous system has been 'fooled' into a state
of emergency. It should be remembered that the automatic nervous system's responses are crude and primitive,
since this mechanism developed very early in human
evolution to protect us from wild animals and other
obvious dangers. It was not designed to make fine judg-
ments about how dangerous a supermarket may be! Once
it is triggered, the full fight or flight response occurs, with
the automatic nervous system 'assuming' that if the
tension level is so high, the situation must be dangerous.
Because the actual final stress is only minor, the person
is not consciously aware of any immediate danger in the
environment. As a result, the person experiencing panic
for the first time is bewildered by the powerful impulse
to 'fight' or 'run away' and understandably interprets
these weird feelings as signs of going mad or losing

control. The physical sensations (palpitations, sweating, tingling in the hands and feet) seem to have nothing to do with the environment, so that it is natural for her to think that these feelings must be symptoms of some serious physical or mental illness. It is not surprising that once the early attacks have subsided, sufferers are left with strong lingering fears that they are ill, about to die or experiencing early signs of mental illness. Background factors keep these fears alive and even make them worse. If a person is prone to catastrophic thinking then the fears of imminent death or loss of control will be magnified. Every physical sensation is taken to be a sign that the 'illness' is coming back or getting worse.

The situation is made worse by the powerful conditioning effects of having a fight or flight response in a particular situation. To protect you from future 'danger', your nervous system 'remembers' what the situation was in which the emergency reaction occurred: then it 'warns' you by producing early anxiety symptoms every time you approach that or a similar situation. In this way the vicious cycle of fear, avoidance and agoraphobia is set up.

Some ways of 'coping' with the situation in fact make it worse. Some people may become more pressured in their activities under stress and then manage their time poorly, leading to more pressure and anxiety. Others who have a strong need for approval, and thus find it difficult to say 'no' for fear of rejection, may accept too many tasks to compensate for the difficulties caused by fear and panic attacks, and try to meet too many demands. Again, the result is more pressure and more anxiety. Yet others will tend to avoid 'risky' situations or to give up and retreat once they have had their first few panic attacks. They are likely to withdraw into themselves and become despondent, losing their self-esteem and confidence. Others, by contrast, may be so determined to overcome the problem that they force themselves repeatedly into difficult situations without using appropriate techniques to overcome their anxiety. This leads to an escalation of stress, frustration and the likelihood of having further panic attacks.

Social factors

The social crises that lead to a build-up of tension before the onset of panic disorder may continue after the attacks begin, causing the sufferer continuing and increasing stress. Pressures at work or at home may be longstanding and difficult to resolve. The internal stress (worrying about having another panic attack) adds to the external stress at work or at home, leading to a mounting spiral of tension and creating a high risk of panic attacks recurring. To try to cope with immediate problems at work, suffers may give up their social, leisure and sporting activities. Instead of relaxing and enjoying recreational outings with their spouse, partner or family, they bring work home to try to 'get on top' of the pressure. They may not realize that the increasing pressure they are putting themselves under is actually making it more likely that they will suffer further panic attacks. Once this vicious cycle is established, it becomes difficult for panic sufferers to see clearly whether the stress is coming from 'outside.' or 'inside'.

Physical factors

Bouts of illness such as the flu can mimic anxiety and thus intensify panic symptoms. Viral infections cause fever, sweating, tiredness, light-headedness and weakness, so that it is easy for the sufferer of panic disorder to mistake these symptoms for worsening anxiety. As discussed earlier, it is relatively rare for a serious physical illness to mimic panic disorder, but if any such disease is discovered it should be treated actively.

Most of the physical factors that can lead to panic disorder also may keep it going. The hyperventilation-panic cycle, discussed earlier, can strongly increase the risk of further attacks, especially in a person who remains in a state of worry and stress. Poor general health, loss of fitness and inadequate sleep – often provoked by the stress of having panic attacks – only make the situation worse. A pressured lifestyle increases the risk of overexertion (e.g. running up stairs to get to your office early), producing sensations such as sweating, rapid heart rate and heavy breathing which can be mislabelled as panic, making the sufferer believe that the situation is worse than it really is. In such circumstances the sufferer may try to dampen symptoms or improve performance by using alcohol, drugs or other stimulants. As discussed earlier, the risk of complicating panic disorder by misusing alcohol or drugs cannot be overemphasized.

PANIC

PERPETUATING
FACTORS

Psychological factors	*Social factors*	*Physical factors*
ongoing stress	chronic stress	hyperventilation
poor coping with stress	pressured lifestyle	poor sleep
		overexertion
fear of illness	family tension	poor general health
fear of further panic attacks	reduction in leisure time	alcohol
negative thinking:	social isolation	drugs
• catastrophic thinking		
• loss of sense of control		
• loss of self-esteem and confidence		

Figure 2. What keeps panic disorder going: a summary

4

How can panic disorder and agoraphobia be treated?

There have been impressive advances in the treatment of panic disorder since the early 1980s. Several carefully designed studies, together with the extensive clinical experience of experts, indicate that with guided practice most sufferers of panic disorder should make a good recovery. Most of the studies conducted have investigated people who have full symptoms of panic disorder, with or without agoraphobia, but there is no reason to suspect that sufferers of less intense panic attacks will not benefit from these techniques. Treatments that have been evaluated across the world include both psychological interventions, particularly techniques which fall under the broad heading of *cognitive behavioral therapy*, and medications, especially using drugs called the tricyclics and the minor tranquilizers (or benzodiazepines).

The emphasis in Part Two of this book is on a cognitive behavioral approach to self-management. In this chapter a brief outline of relevant medications is first provided: more details can be sought from your doctor. Then the cognitive behavioral approach to therapy is outlined. Other methods of therapy offered around the world include traditional psychotherapy based on psychoanalytical principles; family and marital therapy; and various newer psychotherapies. Readers who wish to inquire about those approaches should discuss the possibilities with their doctor or local mental health service

Medications

Experts differ somewhat in their views about the use of medication for panic disorder. Several studies have shown that medications such as the minor tranquilizers (known as the benzodiazepines) and the tricyclics (traditionally used to treat depression) are effective in reducing symptoms of panic. Those therapists who are concerned about the use of medications raise the following issues:

- many sufferers do not wish to take medication;
- medications have side-effects which can themselves be upsetting;
- some medications encourage dependence after long use, and the ensuing withdrawal symptoms may mimic anxiety;
- taking medication does not help the sufferer gain control over the problem;
- people may suffer a relapse after they cease taking medication;
- in some cases, medication may interfere with attempts to learn techniques of self-control.

Medications may be useful in the short term, for example where anxiety is very severe, where the person is not in a state to commence practicing anxiety management techniques, or in other circumstances that make it difficult to use psychological treatments. Wherever possible, however, non-drug approaches to treating panic disorder should also be attempted, to lessen the sufferer's need to take medication. Where medication is used, it should be under the direct supervision of an experienced medical practitioner. This will ensure that the dose is carefully monitored, that possible side-effects will be detected and that the drug can be gradually withdrawn over time if appropriate.

Types of medication

Tricyclic medication

Tricyclic medications are a group of drugs that were first introduced to treat depression, but have subsequently been found to be effective in the treatment of several other conditions including panic disorder, obsessive-compulsive disorder and chronic pain. Donald Klein observed that the tricyclic imipramine reduced symptoms of panic disorder, and further studies have confirmed the effectiveness of imipramine and related tricyclic medications in treating panic. These drugs appear to increase the effect of certain natural chemicals in the brain, called neurotransmitters, which transmit signals across nerves. Reactivating these nerve pathways appears to stabilize anxiety.

These medications generally are taken at night, and the dose is increased gradually. Beneficial effects can take between one and three weeks to become apparent. Possible side-effects include sedation (which is why the dose is better taken at night), a dry mouth, blurred vision and, occasionally, dizziness on standing up. Sometimes people with panic disorder notice that they feel jittery and tense when they start to take medication of this type. By building up the dose very gradually, the side-effects can be minimized; and if they do occur, they tend to subside after a few weeks of treatment. Although these drugs are safe for those who are healthy, they may not be suitable for some people suffering from major physical diseases such as heart or kidney problems. Also, there are risks if excessive doses are taken, or if the medication is taken in combination with alcohol or other drugs.

Newer groups of medications used in the treatment of panic disorder which also increase the effects of neurotransmitters in the brain include the SSRIs or selective serotonin reuptake inhibitors (e.g. fluoxetine, paroxetine and sertraline) and the reversible MAOIs or mono-amine oxidase inhibitors (e.g. moclobemide). They tend to be safer for people with physical illnesses than the older drugs and cause fewer side-effects. They are usually taken in the morning since they may cause sleep disturbance in the initial stages of treatment. Other possible side-effects include headaches and nausea, but these tend to subside after the first few weeks. Although these drugs show promise, further studies are needed to confirm that they are useful in panic disorder.

Benzodiazepines or minor tranquilizers

The group of medications called the benzodiazepines are commonly prescribed for panic disorder. The most extensively studied drug in this group for panic disorder is called alprazolam, which is as effective as imipramine. It does have side-effects, of which the most important are sedation and interference with concentration. The main drawbacks of this group of medications are the development of tolerance – in other words, over time the dose may need to be increased to achieve the same effect – their tendency to cause dependence, and the risk of unpleasant effects if the medication is withdrawn too rapidly. These withdrawal effects can mimic panic symptoms, thus discouraging people from attempting to stop taking the medication. Reducing the dose should therefore be monitored closely by an experienced doctor. Many doctors favor using these drugs selectively and for a short period only, with the aim of substituting non-drug methods to control anxiety in the long term.

Other medications

Occasionally, doctors will prescribe a beta-blocker (which is usually used to treat high blood pressure and some other heart problems) to counter some of the physical symptoms of panic, especially tremor and rapid heartbeat. This medication has little effect on the psychological symptoms that occur during a panic attack, although some people find that when the physical symptoms are less prominent they are able to cope more effectively with their attacks.

Buspirone is another agent that has been successfully used to treat various types of anxiety, though most often 'generalized' anxiety rather than panic. As with the anti-depressant medications discussed above, the effect may be delayed, so that the medication needs to be taken for a few weeks to achieve maximum benefit.

Psychological treatments

Several types of psychological approaches are used for the treatment of panic disorder. The techniques outlined in this book are drawn mainly from the principles of cognitive behavioral therapy, since these approaches have been used extensively over the last few decades and researchers have shown convincingly that the methods – if systematically applied – can make a major impact on problems such as panic and agoraphobia. One of the great advantages of these techniques is that they lend themselves well to a self-help approach which emphasizes self-directed practice and methods for exerting self-control over anxiety.

Cognitive behavioral therapy is based on the principles of *learning theory*, which suggests that many behaviors, and the symptoms that they cause, develop as a result of a repeated pattern of responses to conditions in our environment. In other words, we can develop faulty habits in the way we respond to environmental stress, and these learnt behaviors can in themselves lead to symptoms of distress. If these habits can be *learnt*, then it is possible to *unlearn* them and to *relearn* better methods of coping which do not cause distress and difficulties in living. Cognitive behavioral therapy thus offers the sufferer from panic disorder and agoraphobia the possibility of learning by practice and repetition new ways of dealing with difficult situations and the anxieties that they may cause.

As we have already seen, there are several types of learning. Unhelpful learning may lead to habits which produce symptoms of anxiety. Conditioning can occur, so that a particular response such as extreme fear is produced every time you are exposed to a particular situation. For example, if you repeatedly experience panic in a supermarket, then you become conditioned to feel afraid whenever you go into a supermarket, even if you are not actually being threatened. By avoiding the situation, you also avoid the unpleasant emotions associated with fear. The relief you feel further reinforces avoidance of the situation and increases the risk that your agoraphobic symptoms will worsen. Once established, avoidance can be difficult toundo. That is why the method that is used has to be practiced systematically over time. The method is called *gradual exposure* or *systematic desensitization*, and involves approaching feared situations in a step-by-step manner, giving yourself time to allow any feelings of fear and anxiety to settle before leaving. This ensures that *counter-conditioning* occurs: that is, the connection between the situation and the fear response is broken, and instead the situation or place becomes associated increasingly with feeling at ease. Of course, this transition usually takes time and practice to achieve, and over-rapid exposure to feared situations may make the anxiety worse.

That is why the exposure needs to be gradual, starting from the least anxiety-provoking situations to those that cause most fear. Regular practice as part of a systematic program is also important to achieve good results: if the exercises are practiced only occasionally, then there is time for the old habits to strengthen again between attempts.

Our inner thought processes or what are known as *cognitive mechanisms* also play an important role in learning. The *A-B-C* model is useful in understanding this form of learning. *A* refers to the situation, place or event in the outside world, *B* to the way we interpret or think about that event and *C* to our emotional or behavioral response. According to cognitive theory, component *B* is critical to human learning: often it is not the outside event itself that makes us feel depressed or anxious, but the way we interpret that event. We can all see from our own experience that the same event affects people in very different ways. If the boss is in an angry mood, some workers may immediately assume that it is their fault, that they have done something wrong and that they must work harder to mollify the boss. Others may simply shrug and assume that something probably has gone wrong in the boss's private life and that her bad mood has nothing to do with them. Predictably, the first group will become anxious, worried, and guilty, and might work longer hours, whereas the second group will simply continue with their normal work in the expectation that the boss's mood will improve.

Applying cognitive techniques helps us to identify, reconsider and if necessary alter unrealistically negative interpretations of events or situations. Often we make ourselves anxious by 'overpredicting': that is, we anticipate the worst outcome. In other words, even before we enter a situation or place, our thought processes may be warning us that we will become stressed or anxious, or may even have a panic attack. As a result we fear the situation and avoid it. By monitoring and systematically trying to change these negative thoughts, it is possible to reduce the anticipatory anxiety that may build up into a panic attack. Cognitive techniques also allow you to challenge the typical catastrophic thoughts associated with panic, so that it is possible to shorten an attack and to reduce its impact on your emotional state.

Cognitive behavioral therapy therefore allows the sufferer from panic and agoraphobia to recognize and examine exactly how symptoms are produced and to practice systematic methods to prevent or control these symptoms. By approaching the problem from both a cognitive and a behavioral perspective, the sufferer is able to use a combination of techniques to beat the problem.

In summary, the principles guiding recovery involve:

- understanding the nature of panic attacks and panic disorder and the 'fear of fear' and 'fear of illness' cycles;
- learning the skills required to combat the symptoms of panic attacks and anxiety;
- practicing exercises to replace unhelpful or catastrophic thoughts with more helpful ones;
- developing an approach to dealing with bodily

symptoms that trigger anxiety and learning to evaluate more realistically the meaning of those sensations;

- gradually facing the situations previously avoided in order to overcome agoraphobia.

Combination treatment

For some sufferers, a combination of psychological techniques (especially cognitive behavioral approaches) and appropriate medications may be useful. A person who is suffering from severe or frequent panic attacks may have such high levels of anxiety that he is not able to put psychological techniques into practice straight away. In these situations, it may be helpful to consider medication in the short term to reduce the levels of anxiety sufficiently for cognitive behavioral strategies to be applied. It may then be possible to reduce the medication gradually, using cognitive behavioral treatment to maintain improvement.

Will treatment help?

Sufferers from panic disorder may be afraid that they will never recover. This fear in itself can hamper recovery. Fortunately, over 80 per cent of people (some studies indicate even higher rates) report significant and lasting improvement from using cognitive behavioral approaches. In other words, once people with panic disorder learn how to control and then prevent panic attacks, they can remain symptom-free for long periods, often several years. Even if they experience some symptoms at a later stage, these usually are less severe and more easily controlled. So it *is* worthwhile helping yourself by learning to manage your anxiety. You will feel the benefits not only immediately, but for years to come.

5

A short technical note

Although agoraphobia has been recognized for a long time, it was not until 1980 that panic disorder was added to the American classificatory system, the *Diagnostic and Statistical Manual of Mental Disorders*, third edition *(DSM-III)*. Prior to that, panic disorder was considered to be part of 'anxiety neurosis', which included many different types of anxiety.

The definition of panic attacks and panic disorder

The fourth and most recent edition of the *DSM* *(DSM-IV)* requires that at least four of a list of thirteen symptoms be present for a panic attack to be diagnosed (see Table 1). Most sufferers experience more than four symptoms, and the same person may experience different types of symptoms on different occasions. In order to fulfil the criteria for panic disorder, sufferers must have regular panic attacks *and* have a period of at least one month in which they fear having further panic attacks (see Table 2).

The definition of agoraphobia

Panic disorder is classified by the American Psychiatric Association as occurring with or without agoraphobia. The defining features of agoraphobia are set out in Table 3. Some people may suffer from agoraphobia without ever suffering from panic disorder, or they may suffer from some other underlying disorder such as depression.

Table 1: The defining features of panic attacks

A panic attack is a discrete period of intense fear or discomfort in which four (or more) of the following symptoms develop abruptly and reach a peak within ten minutes:

1. Palpitations, pounding heart or accelerated heart rate
2. Sweating
3. Trembling or shaking
4. Sensations of shortness of breath or smothering
5. Feeling of choking
6. Chest pain or discomfort
7. Nausea or abdominal distress
8. Feeling dizzy, unsteady, light-headed or faint
9. Derealization (feelings of unreality) or depersonalization (being detached from oneself)
10. Fear of losing control or going crazy
11. Fear of dying
12. Paresthesias (numbness or tingling sensations)
13. Chills or hot flushes

Source: adapted from American Psychiatric Association, *DSM-IV*, 1994.

Table 2: The defining features of panic disorder

Both (1) and (2) must be present:
1. Recurrent unexpected panic attacks (see Table 1); and
2. At least one of the attacks is followed by one month (or more) of one (or more) of the following:
   (a) persistent concern about having additional attacks;
   (b) worry about the implications of the attack or its consequences (e.g. losing control, having a heart attack, 'going crazy');
   (c) a significant change in behavior related to the attacks.

Source: adapted from American Psychiatric Association, *DSM-IV*, 1994.

Table 3: The defining features of agoraphobia

Anxiety about being in places or situations from which escape might be difficult (or embarrassing) or in which help may not be available in the event of having a panic attack

The situations are avoided or else are endured with marked distress or with anxiety about having a panic attack, or require the presence of a companion

Source: adapted from American Psychiatric Association, *DSM-IV*, 1994.

How common are panic disorder and agoraphobia?

About 10 per cent of the general population experience at least one unexpected panic attack in their lifetime. Although figures vary, approximately 2–6 per cent of the population suffer from panic disorder at some time in their lives. About two-thirds of sufferers are female. About 60 per cent of people with panic disorder also develop agoraphobia.

Most commonly, panic disorder begins in the mid to late twenties, although it can begin at any age. Many sufferers do not seek treatment at all; those who do usually do so in the mid-thirties.

Panic, agoraphobia and other anxiety disorders

Panic attacks can occur in specific situations and be caused by other anxiety disorders. For example, people may develop panic symptoms when exposed to specific objects or situations (spiders, heights, air travel), in which case they are suffering from specific *phobias*. People who suffer from *social phobia* experience intense anxiety when in a situation of scrutiny, for example when eating in public or having to make a speech. People with *obsessive-compulsive disorder* may become very anxious if they see a risk of becoming contaminated, or if they cannot complete their rituals of checking, counting or washing. Those suffering from *post-traumatic stress disorder* following a life-threatening shock may startle easily or become extremely anxious if exposed to reminders of their trauma.

The syndrome known as *generalized anxiety disorder* (GAD) may be associated with panic disorder. GAD is a condition in which a person suffers from anxiety symptoms most of the time and tends to worry excessively or unnecessarily about many things. In its pure form it does not include acute attacks of panic. While there may be a great deal of overlap between the two conditions, most research studies have found differences between them in terms of family history, inheritance patterns and response to specific treatments.

Although all these conditions belong to the 'family' of anxiety disorders, and they may overlap or coexist in the same person, it is worth trying to be accurate in diagnosing which form of anxiety is most prominent. General stress management techniques are valuable in most forms of anxiety, but it is increasingly apparent that specific techniques are most useful for each disorder. In other words, the closer the match between diagnosis and management, the better the outcome.

After working through the self-help program for panic disorder and agoraphobia in Part Two of this book, you may find it useful to gather more information about the treatment of general stress and anxiety symptoms. Refer to the self-help book on stress management in this series, or consult your family doctor or local mental health service for other treatment programs.

PART TWO

Dealing with Panic Attacks: A Self-Help Manual

Introduction

At first, when the attacks started, I thought they would just go away by themselves. When they lasted for a few months, I began to realize that I had to do something about them. I never considered that this would require psychological treatment. The symptoms seemed so physical, like I was having a heart attack or something, and I just wanted a fast cure. I wanted to find a way to stop the attacks immediately.

Lorraine

There are a number of techniques that can be used to control and even eliminate panic attacks. Some sufferers may not be aware that such techniques are available or effective. Others may give up practicing the techniques because they expect immediate results which do not materialize, or because they feel unsupported in their efforts.

A self-help approach

The important message is that it is possible to learn effective skills to manage panic. These skills may be acquired from a self-management book such as this one; for some people, the book may best be used in conjunction with more intensive treatment provided by a professional in mental health. Either way, this book should offer a first step in combating panic attacks and agoraphobia, whether or not further professional help is sought.

Who will benefit from this self-help manual?

Reading this self-help manual should benefit a range of people who are interested in finding out more about panic disorder and agoraphobia. There are broadly four groups of people who should find this book helpful:

1. Those people currently suffering from panic attacks, with or without agoraphobia, who are interested in learning specific skills to combat anxiety. For some, this book may be sufficient on its own to teach them the necessary skills to control panic symptoms and agoraphobia. Those already involved in treatment programs should find that this book is a useful supplement to their individual or group treatments.

2. Those who have suffered from panic attacks in the past and who wish to learn techniques to prevent the symptoms coming back. Detecting early symptoms and knowing how to combat them will help the ex-sufferer to feel confident about preventing relapse.

3. Those who are familiar with the basic principles of anxiety management but who have not incorporated these skills into a structured program. If skills are used in a haphazard manner or without the

necessary practice, they are likely to be less effective. The six-step program outlined in this book provides a systematic method for overcoming and preventing panic attacks.

4. Relatives and friends of sufferers who wish to gain a fuller understanding of panic disorder. People who are close to sufferers often want to help but feel unable to do so because they do not know what to do or what to suggest. Relatives and friends who take an active interest can be very helpful as long as the advice and support they offer are appropriate and constructive.

Who should seek further assistance?

Not all people with symptoms of panic will be helped by this book, and some may need additional assistance. Special attention will be necessary for six groups of people in particular:

1. Those who have any of the rare physical disorders that mimic panic attacks. This manual is designed for the treatment of panic attacks that stern from stress-related psychological factors. In Part One of this book we described a number of medical conditions that (although rare) may produce symptoms similar to panic. If there is any suspicion that you may have one of these conditions you should consult your family doctor.

2. Those suffering from severe agoraphobia, especially if that disorder is unrelated to symptoms of panic.

These people need a thorough assessment and intensive assistance from an experienced mental health professional. This book is intended for people suffering primarily from panic disorder who may or may not have some degree of agoraphobia. If avoidance of situations or places is your main difficulty then you should consult your doctor or your local mental health service for further advice.

3. Those suffering from severe depression associated with panic disorder, who may not have the necessary motivation to work through a self-help book on their own. They may need to seek treatment for their depressive illness before they can start to work actively to combat anxiety symptoms such as panic attacks. Depressed persons may require antidepressant medication to life their mood and to enable them to concentrate enough to embark on this program. A brief guide to the management of depression is provided at the end of the book.

4. Those who lack the confidence to work on their own, who may decide at the outset that a self-help program such as this is not enough. If practice of the suggested techniques is halfhearted, the results will not be satisfactory. If your motivation is low through lack of confidence, working with a therapist may help you to summon up the necessary energy to embark on change.

5. Those who have strong resistance to lifestyle change. In some cases, especially when panic disorder has become entrenched, sufferers may reorganize their

lives to accommodate the problem. The notion that recovery will require a change in lifestyle can seem threatening and may be actively avoided. Panic disorder and agoraphobia can become a way of life which is difficult to overcome. A more thorough review of the motivation to change may be needed, with the help of an expert therapist.

6. Those for whom panic attacks and agoraphobia are only one aspect of wider emotional, social or personality problems. For example, people who respond to stress by misusing drugs or alcohol may need to seek counselling for substance abuse before (or at the same time as) trying to overcome panic disorder. For a person who has panic attacks and is also severely mentally disturbed, for example in a state of severe depression or psychosis, this book will be of little use and the help of a mental health professional should be sought.

Early hurdles to self-management

Understanding the factors that may undermine efforts at self-help can be helpful in overcoming these obstacles.

Fear of change

The six-step programme that follows this chapter recommends ways of changing those elements of your life that cause and perpetuate panic attacks and agoraphobia. For many people, these changes in lifestyle and daily routine may seem daunting. It may seem safer to keep things as they are – indeed, the very thought of change may cause a temporary increase in anxiety! It is important to confront the reality that although limitations in your lifestyle – like avoiding going to the city or taking a train – may make your life more 'comfortable,' in the long term such restrictions are very disabling.

Lack of support

Sometimes, friends or relatives whom you tell of your intention to pursue a self-help program may be discouraging. Occasionally, others may be dismissive and express disbelief that a book can help. Relatives may be overly cautious or protective. Those close to you may be fearful of any changes that they may have to make in their own lifestyles once your condition starts to improve. Whatever the reason for their lack of support, it is important to realize that the choice to change is an individual decision that you make for yourself. Although it is helpful to elicit the support of friends and family, it is not critical to your success that you obtain the support of everyone around you before you start putting this self-help program into practice.

Making a commitment to change

As a first step, it may be useful for you to consider the potential benefits and drawbacks of overcoming panic attacks and agoraphobia. Making a list and rating each item from -10 to +10 in terms of its importance in improving lifestyle may help to focus your thinking on the reasons for making changes. A minus score indicates a negative impact of making a lifestyle change; a score of 0 indicates 'no effect on lifestyle' or a 'neutral' effect of making a change; and a plus score indicates a beneficial effect. An example of this exercise is shown in Table 1.

Table 1: Working out the benefits of change			
Benefits of change	Impact on lifestyle (-10 to +10)	Consequence of no change	Impact on lifestyle (-10 to +10)
Able to go to supermarket alone	+7	Have to wait for friend/mother to go out with me	-3
Able to find a job	+9	Forced to stay at home and watch TV	-5
Able to go to the movies with friends	+5	Have to wait for DVD version to be released	-4
Could throw a dinner party	+8	Can't socialize with groups of friends	-4

Listing the benefits of change in this way gives you a reminder of why it is so important to overcome panic attacks and agoraphobia. Rereading your list may also help you when, at times, the effort to change seems too great, or if there have been temporary setbacks in your program.

Overcoming panic attacks must be regarded as a worthwhile and necessary pursuit, as important as any other commitment, such as pursuing a career, studying for a diploma or caring for your family. People who want to overcome panic attacks and agoraphobia may wish for an immediate 'magic cure' or a 'fast-acting pill' that will get rid of their anxiety symptoms immediately. If it were that easy, then you would not be reading this book! In reality, beating panic disorder and/or agoraphobia requires time, some hard work and a determination to succeed. If you are prepared to treat each small success as a step towards overcoming the problem, and if you accept that there may be small setbacks along the way, then you eventually will succeed.

Dealing with setbacks

Setbacks may occur in any treatment program. At the beginning it can be difficult to control all sources of stress and all triggers of panic attacks. Sometimes a number of small stresses occur in rapid succession, making it difficult to implement the intended changes to your daily life. A single major life event, such as the death of a family member or a serious illness in a close friend, may result in a recurrence of panic attacks and agoraphobia. There are also particular times in people's lives when setbacks are more likely to occur. For example, overwork, poor sleep or a viral infection may cause anxiety symptoms to flare up. If these stresses occur before anxiety management skills have been mastered it becomes harder to control symptoms.

The way in which these minor setbacks are dealt with can make a great impact on long-term progress. You may feel totally demoralized by a minor setback and decide that it is useless to go on with the program; you may then give up trying and resign yourself to becoming increasingly agoraphobic and dependent on the people around you. On the other hand, you may decide that minor setbacks provide the opportunity to practice your anxiety management skills in new situations, and thus learn to regard new forms of stress as a challenge rather than as a catastrophe.

The urge to quit

For most people, there will be several moments during this program when they feel like quitting. Falling back on the same safe routines, however restrictive they are, may seem more comfortable than keeping up the effort required to change.

If you are faced with the urge to quit, try one or more of the following:

- reading through your 'benefits of change' table (see Table 1) to remind yourself that it is worth continuing;
- talking to a close, supportive friend or family member about the benefits of overcoming anxiety, again to remind yourself of the reasons for continuing with the self-help program;
- accepting that a break in the program is not a disaster and being willing to return to an earlier step when you feel ready to begin again;
- recognizing that you may have tried to progress through the program too rapidly and that you have not had enough time to practice the skills introduced

in the earlier stages; slowing down progress from one step to the next may help consolidate what you have learnt;
* visualizing or imagining a panic-free lifestyle and all the activities that then will become possible to rediscover the incentive to continue.

Self-questions that undermine your efforts

You may find you ask yourself the same self-defeating questions over and over again, thereby undermining your confidence. It is worth considering some of these at the outset.

Why can't I just stop panicking?

This question is asked regularly by people with panic disorder. Although the first panic attack may have occurred out of the blue, it is important to realize that the stresses that eventually led to the onset of panic attacks may have been building up over several months or even years. Your body's physiological processes have been adapting gradually as your levels of tension have been rising. Once the 'habit' of triggering panic has set in, it takes time to reset the body's mechanisms to a normal level, where the prevailing degree of tension is not so close to the 'fight or flight' trigger. Thus a process of physical 'realignment' must occur; you cannot just 'decide' not to panic any more.

The expectation that panic attacks can be stopped simply by willpower places unnecessary pressure on the sufferer to get better quickly. Sheer effort of will without the skills to apply the necessary techniques unfortunately does not automatically guarantee success. Such expectations of immediate recovery lead people to become disappointed and to blame themselves, creating additional pressure. This added pressure may fuel further panic attacks and create more feelings of demoralization.

Nearly everyone who has had a panic attack remembers what the first episode felt like, even years later. It is a powerful experience that usually sensitizes sufferers to any sensations that remind them of that first attack. Trying to forget the initial experience of panic is difficult and unhelpful. It is more important to place those memories in the past, where they are no longer threatening.

Repeated panic attacks undermine self-confidence, so that after a series of attacks you become unsure of yourself and worry about embarrassing yourself in front of others. Previously easy tasks such as driving through heavy traffic, waiting for a bus or buying tickets to a movie become major ordeals. Many sufferers find themselves having to rely excessively on other people; or they may feel isolated and incompetent. Regaining self-confidence usually takes time and patience as you slowly attempt to overcome your anxiety in different situations. As with most practical tasks, some attempts will be successful while some may be disappointing. Eventually, as more tasks are successfully accomplished, self-confidence will improve, but the process is a gradual one.

Why am I different?

You may notice that your relationships with people close to you have changed since you began to have panic attacks. Unfortunately, some of these changes may not be healthy or satisfying. Sufferers may notice that their partners, children or friends treat them differently because they cannot leave the house or participate in social activities without experiencing distress. Some friends may even desert them. Relatives may offer simple and thoughtless 'advice', or even try to bully sufferers into overcoming their anxiety and avoidance behavior. After anxiety and panic attacks have subsided, some former sufferers notice that their relationships with others have not changed accordingly: that is, other people continue to treat them as if they were still suffering from panic disorder. This may be especially so if they have reorganized aspects of their own lifestyles to accommodate the sufferer. Re-educating friends and family to behave differently may take time and patience.

Not all the after-effects of suffering from panic disorder are negative. Often, people who have suffered from panic disorder and agoraphobia are more sensitive to other people's distress and tension and better able to understand the difficulties and anxieties that others may experience. They are usually able to suggest helpful techniques and skills to assist those around them to control anxiety.

Many of the skills used to overcome panic attacks and agoraphobia can be applied to other stress-related problems. These skills can be a sound investment for dealing with other stressful events that may occur later in life.

About the self-help program

The program outlined in this manual is designed to provide the basic skills necessary to control panic attacks and to overcome agoraphobia. Several years of research and clinical experience have shown that the techniques outlined here are effective. Not all the skills presented will be appropriate for everyone, but most people will find at least some of them helpful. It is best to reserve judgment as to whether each step will be of benefit to you until you have practiced the techniques for some time. Like most skills, anxiety management techniques take time to learn, and the benefits may not be apparent immediately.

It is possible for most people to work through this manual in six to eight weeks. This is only a rough guide since it is most important to work through the six steps systematically and not to progress to the next step until the previous ones have been practiced and mastered. Some people may need longer than a few weeks. It is important not to work through the program as fast as possible but to understand the techniques and to practice the skills, no matter how long it takes.

How to use this manual

The best approach to using this manual is first to skim through the six steps, getting an idea of the skills and tasks involved. This will make the whole program less formidable and should reduce anxiety about what may lie ahead. Once you have familiarized yourself with the manual in this way, then work through each of the six steps in turn, first reading right through the step before attempting the tasks or exercises suggested. Make sure you have grasped each step and are comfortable practicing the techniques it introduces before moving on to the next step. When you have worked through the six steps systematically, you may want to reread the manual to reinforce the skills you have learnt.

Recruiting a helper

You may wish to get a friend or relative to help you through the six-step program. This can be a good way to make sure that you practice the skills and to keep you motivated to work through the book. A reliable helper can support you through those difficult times when you may be tempted to give up, or become temporarily discouraged. He or she can also help you to acknowledge your successes, especially when you may not recognize them as significant achievements yourself. On the other hand, there will come a point when you need to carry out tasks independently to achieve full recovery. This needs to be recognized by you and your helper in advance, and you will need to discuss the issue with each other regularly so that the point of independence is not delayed.

Step 1. Recognizing when you are anxious and identifying panic triggers
(learning accurately to monitor physical and psychological symptoms of panic and sources of stress)

⬇

Step 2. Lifestyle factors that may be contributing to anxiety and panic attacks
(changing aspects of lifestyle to reduce the likelihood of panic attacks occurring)

⬇

Step 3. Controlling panic attacks
(learning techniques to control and eliminate panic attacks)

⬇

Step 4. Changing unhelpful thinking styles
(identifying, challenging and learning to change negative thinking styles)

⬇

Step 5. Reducing sensitivity to physical sensations
(learning not to be fearful of 'normal' physical sensations)

⬇

Step 6. Putting these skills into practice
(overcoming agoraphobia and establishing a new lifestyle)

Figure 1. The six steps of the self-help program outlined in this manual

The six steps

The six steps outlined in this self-help program are as follows.

In **Step 1** you will get to know your particular stress symptoms and to identify the 'triggers' that set off your panic attacks. It focuses on learning to monitor symptoms so that you will be able to distinguish between actual anxiety symptoms and those symptoms that seem like anxiety but are really due to other factors.

Step 2 focuses on lifestyle factors that may be increasing the risk of panic attacks. In particular, it examines the importance of diet, exercise, sleep and relaxation to your psychological health.

Step 3 introduces some specific techniques to control panic attacks and other anxiety symptoms when they occur. Being able to control these symptoms will increase your self-confidence and should enable you to tackle situations that you may have been avoiding.

Step 4 considers the negative thinking patterns that may be contributing to anxiety symptoms. There is little doubt that our attitude to and thoughts about ourselves, our bodily sensations and outside events can influence the way we feel and behave. By changing some of these attitudes, it is possible to change the way we feel about ourselves, our lives and our feelings, thus influencing the levels of anxiety and stress we experience.

Step 5 examines the way in which physical sensations trigger fearful thinking and thus increase the risk of further panic. Labelling physical sensations more accurately helps to reduce this tendency.

Step 6, the last step in the program, focuses on applying skills in a wide range of situations to overcome agoraphobia and to establish a healthy lifestyle. Learning to control anxiety and to overcome panic disorder means more than just keeping symptoms at bay: it eventually means enjoying your life to the full and not focusing constantly on the fear of having another panic attack.

A review section at the end of each step will help you to monitor your improvement and to set the pace for further progress. You may need to re-read certain sections or re-attempt some exercises before you progress to the next step.

Some advice about eliminating anxiety symptoms

Before you start working through the six steps, it may be helpful to consider the following points. You may also find it useful to read this section again as you work through each of the six steps.

Normal anxiety and panic

This program is aimed at helping you to stop having panic attacks in situations such as shopping, driving or waiting your turn at a bank; but remember that there are some situations where sensations identical to panic are entirely normal. For example, some fairground rides such as the roller-coaster or Big Dipper excite people by stimulating feelings which are very similar to panic but which are enjoyable – for some! Heightened tension is also normal and indeed necessary to ensure that you perform at your best in testing situations such as during examinations or while giving a talk. And if you were to stand in front of an oncoming truck you would experience symptoms of arousal and fear which would be normal – and part of the 'fight or flight response' discussed earlier. Even after you have mastered all the techniques for controlling panic attacks and eliminating anxiety symptoms, some situations will still evoke these powerful emotions. It is worth bearing this in mind: your goal is not to eliminate anxiety completely. It is important to set realistic goals for yourself in managing your anxiety and in overcoming panic attacks.

Preventing anxiety and panic attacks from developing

Most people find that it is easier to stop a panic attack when it is in its early stages than to try to bring it to an end when it is already in full swing.

At the first sign of panic, it is important to apply the techniques you have learnt without delay. In time and with regular practice, these skills will come into play almost automatically, so that controlling the symptoms before they escalate becomes increasingly easier.

A final note

I kept surprising myself how easy it was to do the things that I previously feared. There were so many changes in my lifestyle once I started going out again. I could drive around, visit my friends, pick up the kids from school and go shopping. Best of all, I could start looking for a job, something I've always wanted to do but couldn't consider because of my panic attacks. My relationship with my husband has improved because we don't fight like we used to about my reliance on him. I've even started going out to the club with my girlfriends every Wednesday night. I really feel like I am living again.

Joan

At all times, try to keep in mind that you are embarking on this program for yourself, for your future lifestyle and for the people you care about. There may be several times during the program when you feel like giving up. When these low periods occur, try to keep in mind all the positive changes to your lifestyle and to your relationships that overcoming panic disorder and agoraphobia will deliver.

Step 1

Recognizing when you are anxious and identifying panic triggers

It may seem strange to have to learn about symptoms of anxiety when you have suffered from them for a long time. Most people assume that they can tell the difference between symptoms of anxiety and those caused by physical illness, but many in fact confuse the two. For example, people who suffer from panic attacks often assume that pains in their chest or shortness of breath mean that they are suffering from a physical illness. Though they find it difficult to believe, these symptoms could be caused by anxiety. Also, anxiety symptoms can occur without our being aware of the stresses that give rise to them, seeming to come 'out of the blue', and this can reinforce the belief that they are caused by physical illness.

In panic disorder, especially, it is common for people to think they are suffering from heart disease, a stroke or a brain tumour because of symptoms such as tightness in the chest, difficulty in breathing or strange feelings of unreality. People who suffer from panic attacks may have undergone several physical checkups, cardiac stress tests and numerous blood tests in an attempt to detect a physical cause for their symptoms. It is not uncommon for people suffering from panic attacks to be admitted to hospital for a suspected heart attack.

Pinpointing the symptoms of panic

How, then, do you know when you are experiencing symptoms of panic rather than a physical illness? When health professionals make a diagnosis, they do so by identifying several symptoms that are known to occur together in a regular pattern. In the same way, we tend to recognize our emotions according to a regular pattern of experiences. For example, the emotion of anger is associated with flushing of the face, tension in the jaw, shallow breathing and hostile thoughts. When we feel depressed, we may notice changes such as poor concentration, preoccupation with pessimistic thoughts, disturbed sleep and lack of energy. Of course, no one experiences feelings in exactly the same way or with the same intensity as anyone else. Sometimes the pattern may vary slightly even for the same individual. Nevertheless, when an emotional state develops into a serious problem, the particular pattern of symptoms is sufficiently consistent for a diagnosis to be made.

As an exercise, try describing to yourself the general pattern of symptoms that you have experienced in the past when you felt despondent or depressed.

Your pattern of symptoms when you are depressed:

1.

2.

3.

4.

5.

Extending this exercise to anxiety, we can examine the common patterns of symptoms that people experience when they are stressed or anxious. Once again, it is important to remember that not everyone is the same and that each person will experience a slightly different pattern of symptoms.

Think back to the last time you had symptoms of panic and, in the spaces below, list the major symptoms that you experienced.

Your major symptoms of panic:

1.

2.

3.

4.

5.

Once you have completed the list, try to recall the last three times when you experienced that group of symptoms. On each occasion, did you think you were suffering from a physical illness at the time? Were you baffled by the symptoms, or did you immediately recognize that they were a result of anxiety? The next time you experience these symptoms, try to remember that they are symptoms of anxiety rather than an indication of serious physical illness.

Identifying and monitoring panic triggers

It is worth monitoring your panic attacks over the course of this program so that you can identify major panic triggers. Keep a diary of your panic attacks, noting when and where each attack happens and what the trigger seemed to be, and giving each attack a rating between 0 and 10, where 0 indicates 'minimal symptoms' and 10 indicates the 'worst possible symptoms'. You may also find it useful to rate your level of coping with each panic attack, again using a rating scale from 0 to 10, where 0 indicates the 'poorest level of coping' and 10 your 'best or most effective level of coping'. An example of a few entries in such a diary is given in Figure 2.

Common situations where panic attacks are likely to occur are when driving a car, taking public transport, visiting a busy shopping centre or attending a social function. You may find that there are other situations that are regularly stressful for you.

Date	Situation	Anxiety symptoms (0–10)	Coping (0–10)
4 May	At sister's house with her family	7	4 Had to leave the room
12 May	Waiting in line at the bank	8	2 Left the bank in a hurry
6 June	Taking the dog for a walk	5	6 Managed to complete the walk
10 June	Speaking to my mother on the telephone: I felt criticized	6	7 Continued talking but could not concentrate

Figure 2. Example of diary entries monitoring panic attacks

You also may find that your anxiety is very specific: for example, you may become anxious in the company of some but not all acquaintances.

Use the 'monitoring from for panic attacks' given here to monitor your panic attacks over the next few weeks. (Extra blank copies of this form, and of the other forms used in later steps of the program, are printed at the back of the book.) If you wish, you can add another column and write down how you would have liked to have coped with each particular situation. When rating your level of anxiety, it is important to recognize the normal range of anxiety. Some situations are anxiety-provoking for most people. For example, having to attend a job interview or to give a speech are two situations where some degree of anxiety is to be expected. It may help to discuss your level of anxiety with someone else so that you develop a realistic picture of the types of situations that cause most people to become anxious.

Common sources of anxiety for people with panic disorder

When you describe situations in which you feel anxious, try to be as specific as possible. This will help you to pinpoint particular types of situations that seem to trigger panic attacks. You will probably find that a number of situations can be grouped together because they share certain characteristics or trigger particular fears. Some of these common features are listed below. See how many you can identify as relevant to you and your anxiety symptoms.

Monitoring form for panic attacks

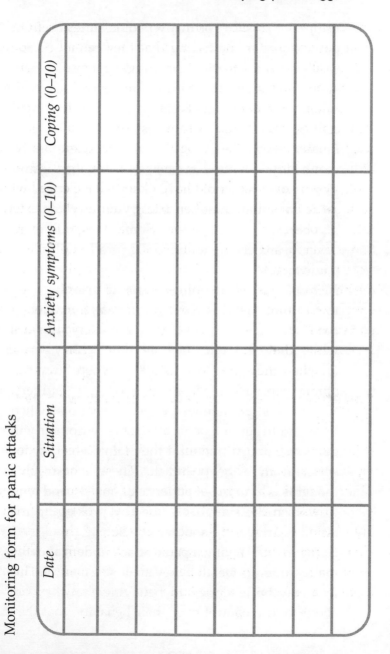

Date	Situation	Anxiety symptoms (0–10)	Coping (0–10)

- *Escape not possible* For many people suffering from panic disorder, the feeling that they cannot escape easily from a situation can trigger intense anxiety symptoms and panic attacks. These situations typically involve crowded places such as shopping centres, sports stadiums or restaurants.

- *Embarrassment* People with panic attacks may be particularly sensitive to others noticing their symptoms of distress. Once you have started experiencing panic symptoms, feeling under scrutiny can add another source of anxiety. Sometimes this extra 'laycr' of anxiety is enough to trigger off a full-blown panic attack.

- *Help not available* People with panic disorder need to feel that 'help' is close by in case they have a panic attack. Some find that their anxiety subsides when they are with people whom they trust, or when they are close to places where they can obtain help, such as a hospital or a doctor's surgery.

- *'Going crazy'* Sometimes people believe that when they start to suffer a panic attack the symptoms will get worse and worse until they faint, 'go crazy' or suffer from a heart attack. These catastrophic thoughts add to the experience of anxiety and tend to worsen the symptoms, thereby prolonging the attack or triggering another attack.

- *Losing control* Having a panic attack understandably makes sufferers feel that they are losing control. This fear may be extended to believing that they are about to lose control over their behavior, that they may run amok, hurt someone or act in a bizarre and embarrassing way. Some situations, like crowded places, intensify this fear because there are people around who would witness such behavior. In reality, panic sufferers do not harm others or act dangerously, but the fear of this, along with the fear of embarrassment noted above, can make the sufferers particularly anxious about certain situations.

Use the checklist below to identify the triggers of anxiety that make your symptoms worse in particular situations and that increase the likelihood of experiencing a panic attack. Perhaps you can think of other repetitive fears or worries that you have whenever you feel anxious; if so, list them on a separate sheet of paper and use the same format to pinpoint which situations are more likely to trigger such thoughts.

Checklist for monitoring situations that trigger common fears

Situation	Escape not possible	Embarrass- ment	Help not available	Going crazy/fear of collapse
_____	☐	☐	☐	☐
_____	☐	☐	☐	☐
_____	☐	☐	☐	☐
_____	☐	☐	☐	☐
_____	☐	☐	☐	☐

Identifying and monitoring agoraphobic symptoms

You may find that you are actually avoiding situations or are entering certain situations only with great reluctance because of your anxiety. What are some of the situations or activities that you have been avoiding? List all those situations or activities in the checklist below. When you have completed the list, rate each of these situations or activities in terms of the difficulty you experience approaching or entering them. Once again, you may wish to use a '0' to '10' scale where '0' indicates 'no anxiety' or 'no difficulty and '10' indicates 'extreme anxiety' or 'severe difficulty'.

Checklist for monitoring situations or activities that you may be avoiding

Situation	Anxiety rating (0–10)
_____	☐
_____	☐
_____	☐
_____	☐
_____	☐
_____	☐

Review of Step 1

After monitoring your panic attacks and avoidance behavior for a few days, you should be able to see particular patterns emerging. Identifying these patterns will help you to focus on applying your anxiety management skills to problematic situations. Ultimately, this will help you to overcome panic attacks and agoraphobia.

- At the beginning of the chapter, you were asked to write down your own pattern of symptoms when you become depressed. Next you were asked to write down your pattern of symptoms when you become anxious. Could you detect a specific pattern of symptoms? Can you list all the symptoms you experience? Next time you experience some or all of these symptoms, try to say to yourself 'these sensations probably mean that I am anxious' rather than jumping to the conclusion that you are suffering from a serious physical illness, going 'crazy', or are about to collapse.
- The second exercise aimed to identify what types of situations and associated fears are likely to trigger panic attacks. Have you noticed that your panic attacks tend to occur at particular times of the day or night? Are there particular situations that are more difficult for you than others? By monitoring your panic attacks, you will be able to focus on some of the factors that may be contributing to your anxieties. For example, if you tend to have panic attacks at the end of the day, it may be that tiredness is playing an important role. If you tend to have attacks at night, you may find that you are dwelling on the day's worries before you go to sleep, or that you are drinking too much coffee before going to bed. Withdrawl symptoms from alcohol misuse could also be a factor.

- The third exercise aimed at helping you become aware of the situations that could worsen your symptoms. You were asked to note the situations which are most likely to trigger fearful thinking. Do you tend to have specific fears and worries in certain situations? What are they? Ways of overcoming these fears and worries will be discussed in detail in Step 4; however, it is helpful to become aware of them early in the program so that you can begin to confront them.

- Exercise four was about monitoring agoraphobic avoidance and rating the severity of your symptoms in those situations. Rating your response in this way will enable you to set realistic targets in trying to confront your fears. By working through the list slowly, from easiest to most difficult, over the course of this program you will gradually be able to overcome your avoidance of those situations.

Try to make a fixed time each week to review your progress and your monitoring forms. Make sure that you are using all these monitoring forms for at least one week before moving on to Step 2, which focuses on lifestyle factors that may be contributing to your panic attacks.

Step 2

Changing lifestyle factors that contribute to panic attacks

Life stress and anxiety: a vicious cycle

A stressful lifestyle can contribute to anxiety symptoms and panic attacks in susceptible people. Most people who suffer from panic attacks can recall several stressful incidents in their lives just before the attacks began. Some of these stresses may continue or worsen with the onset of panic attacks. Problems in any area of life become much more difficult to solve when you are suffering from panic symptoms. Thus you may face a vicious cycle in which life stress makes panic worse and vice versa. For example, if the problem you face relates to your work, then you may respond by working longer hours, skipping meals and neglecting to take exercise. This attempt to 'solve' the backlog in work commitments may instead increase your susceptibility to panic attacks. Or you may find that arguments or difficulties with a spouse or partner have arisen since you began to have panic attacks. Once again a vicious cycle of anxiety symptoms may be set up, as the added relationship stress leads to a worsening of panic attacks, and that puts more pressure on the relationship. The stress may be increased by poor sleep and insufficient time being reserved for leisure and relaxation, raising your level of tension even further.

These everyday stresses can hamper your recovery from panic disorder, especially if you do not have the skills to handle or control your symptoms. Furthermore, if your lifestyle itself is stressful because of poor diet, lack of recreational time or disturbed sleep, then it is likely that your recovery will be slower. On the other hand, you cannot avoid all sources of stress while you recover from panic disorder. A more realistic goal may be to solve problems where you can and to learn how to rid yourself of unnecessary tension by increasing your resilience to life stresses which cannot be fully resolved. A note on problem-solving is added at the end of Step 6.

Step 2 is about building up your resilience to everyday stresses such as those described above. It focuses on simple lifestyle changes that may help to lower your vulnerability to panic attacks, concentrating on four major areas of lifestyle: exercise, nutrition, sleep and relaxation. All four areas are vital in reducing anxiety and in overcoming panic attacks.

Types of stress: the mind–body link

It is useful to divide the common sources of stress into two categories:

- The first type of stress is 'mental stress', which is characterized by fears and worries. You may worry excessively about work, family or friends; or your worries may focus on having another panic attack, coping with public transport, or waiting in line.

- The second type of stress is called 'physical stress', since it relates to your physical health. If your diet is poor and you sleep badly and take too little exercise, then you are placing your body under physical stress. This form of stress can make people more susceptible to fatigue, minor illnesses and irritability. Being 'run down' or physically unfit can make you more vulnerable to other stresses and therefore more likely to suffer from such symptoms as tiredness, headaches and muscle tension.

Because the mind and body are so closely linked, any symptoms of physical ill-health can 'feed back' in a circular fashion resulting in mental ill-health as illustrated in Figure 3. For example, if you are feeling run down and have not slept well for several days, you are more likely to experience poor concentration and irritability. This in turn can affect your self-esteem and confidence, ultimately worsening feelings of anxiety or depression. For some, this kind of physical stress may be enough to trigger panic attacks.

BODY
(symptoms include stomach upsets,
muscle tension and headaches)

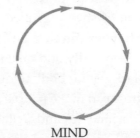

MIND
(symptoms include fears and worries,
poor self-esteem and loss of confidence)

Figure 3. The stress cycle

You may have noticed that after an episode of flu or another physical illness you experience a short period of feeling 'down', exhausted or stressed. This is to be expected, especially if you have not taken enough time off from your usual chores to recover fully. We often have to learn to make time for ourselves, to look after our physical and mental health, and to do so can be a challenge in itself.

Recognizing the link between the mind and body can be helpful in preparing to reduce your levels of stress. Just as chronic physical fatigue can make you more vulnerable to stress, so improving your physical health can make you more resistant to stressful situations. Many people notice that after a good night's sleep followed by a healthy and nutritious breakfast they are able to perform much more effectively in completing their daily chores, whether at home or at work. Similarly, we tend to find that it is difficult to concentrate or apply ourselves efficiently if we are short of sleep or hungry.

Targeting your physical health

As noted above, four main areas of physical stress are targeted in this chapter (exercise, nutrition, sleep and relaxation). You may find that one or several are particularly relevant to you in reducing your vulnerability to stress.

Exercise

Exercising regularly can increase our mental tolerance of stressful situations. Exercise can be a good way of 'working off' tension and boredom, especially if you are spending most of your day at a desk or sitting down in one spot. People who are physically fit also tend to sleep better than those who have not been taking regular exercise. Exercise also can be a good way to meet people or to broaden your daily activities. Joining an exercise club or gym, going for a swim or playing tennis are all ways of becoming fit. Mixing with a new group of people also can take your mind off your worries and concerns, and may help you to direct your attention away from your anxiety symptoms.

Individuals, of course, differ in their physical make-up, in their level of stamina and in the types of exercise they enjoy. Sometimes, exercising with a friend can be both enjoyable and helpful, especially on those days when your motivation may be low. Others enjoy exercising alone. When starting to exercise, make sure you choose a program that you enjoy rather than one that you only carry out as a sense of duty. If you cannot think of any particular exercise you enjoy, think back to when you were younger and probably fitter. What exercises did you enjoy when you were at school? What exercises did you enjoy as a young adult?

If you have not been exercising regularly, avoid over-exerting yourself. Start off with a few minutes of walking every day, then build this up to longer periods of light exercise. If you have not exercised for several months, have a medical check-up before you begin an exercise program.

The following points may help you establish and maintain an exercise routine:

- choose an exercise that you enjoy;
- make sure that you have the right equipment and clothing;
- start with light exercises and only gradually work up to more vigorous ones;
- exercise with a friend if that suits you;
- try to exercise every day or every other day at the same time: establish a routine;
- reward yourself for exercising during the first two weeks if you are just beginning;
- be tolerant of disruptions to your exercise routine: go back to your exercise plan as soon as possible.

Once you notice your fitness level and tolerance level increasing together, of course, this will help to keep you motivated!

People with panic disorder worry that exercise might bring on some of their panic symptoms. While it is likely that exercise will make you feel hot and flushed, raise your breathing and heart rate, and cause you to perspire, it is important to remember that these are normal reactions associated with physical activity. So although these sensations may remind you of having a panic attack, remember that they are not anxiety-related since they have occurred in the context of physical activity. It is helpful to label these physical sensations as healthy, natural bodily responses to exercise.

If you feel hesitant about starting an exercise program, try some very light exercise, like slow walking, every day. Even this will increase your fitness level, and as you become fitter you may notice that you do not feel breathless so often, and are less aware of an increased heart rate. When you feel more confident about your level of fitness, you may then embark on a more vigorous exercise program. Remember that gentle regular exercise is far better than no exercise at all.

Anxiety about leaving the house may limit your choice of exercise at first, especially if you suffer from agoraphobia. If this applies to you, you could ask a friend or member of the family to accompany you; or if this is not possible, you could do some exercise at home until you have built up your confidence to the level where you are ready to leave the house.

Nutrition and Drugs

Physical health, as we have already seen, is closely linked with mental health. Eating sensibly according to your body's needs is a first step in combating stress. If your eating is usually erratic, try to ensure that you have regular meals so that you do not experience wide swings in blood sugar levels. Major fluctuations in blood sugar levels can produce symptoms similar to those of anxiety.

Drinking too much coffee, tea or cola drinks, or eating too much chocolate or foods with high levels of caffeine or other stimulants, can make you feel 'hyped up' and increase the risk of panic attacks. It is not always necessary to drink a lot of tea or coffee to have this effect: if you are one of the few people who are sensitive to even small quantities of these stimulants, you will feel the effect after even moderate amounts.

Nicotine is a powerful stimulant that can increase anxiety. If you smoke, giving up can have a marked beneficial impact on your physical and mental health. If you are a heavy smoker and choose to give up, try to get help from a health professional. He or she can give you a withdrawal program designed to avoid unpleasant symptoms which could worsen your anxiety.

We have already seen how important alcohol can be in provoking panic attacks. Monitoring your alcohol intake and ensuring that you are drinking well below the recommended level for your sex and weight are critical to recovery from panic disorder. Current recommended maximum levels are two standard drinks a day for women and four standard drinks a day for men. (One standard drink equals one glass of wine, one bar measure of spirits or half a pint of beer.)

To summarize, try to establish a healthy diet by following these guidelines:

- make sure you are eating enough fruit and vegetables;
- drink plenty of fluids, especially water, throughout the day;
- if you are trying to lose weight, aim to do so gradually; avoid crash diets and fasting;
- eat regular meals and try not to go for long periods without food;
- try to limit the amount of coffee and tea you drink;
- keep your alcohol consumption below the recommended limit for your sex and weight;
- if you are a smoker, consider quitting with the assistance of a health professional;
- avoid stimulant or mood-altering drugs unless they are prescribed by your doctor.

Sleep

Most people require between seven and nine hours of sleep every night. Some people can make do with less, while others may need more in order to function well. Even members of the same family may have very different sleep requirements. Lack of sleep (or too much sleep) can make you tired, irritable and less able to cope with the demands of daily living. People also differ from one another as to whether they function better in the mornings or in the evenings. Some people find that they can concentrate or work best late at night, others that they work better in the early morning. Individuals also differ in how deeply they sleep. While some may enjoy a long stretch of unbroken sleep, others may have to get up regularly to go to the bathroom or to have a drink during the night: yet both groups may report 'a good night's sleep'. Some people sleep more soundly than others who awaken at every slight sound in the house. Some toss and turn in their sleep, while others hardly move at all throughout the night.

Sleep cycles of this nature are thought to be 'inbuilt', so that trying to alter them substantially, although it is possible, often is difficult to accomplish in the short term. The important point here is that each of us has our own individual sleep habits. There are no fixed 'rules' about the right time to go to bed, how deep your sleep should be, or the number of hours that you need to sleep. What is important is whether

Date	Sleep rating	Problem area(s)
June 3	6	Awakened by a loud storm outside; afraid of thunder and lightning
June 4	4	Had too much to drink the night before
June 5	2	Worried about work, couldn't fall asleep

Figure 4. Example of a sleep diary

you feel refreshed after waking up. If you do not, then you may need to examine your sleep pattern more closely. For example, do you have difficulty falling asleep or staying asleep? Do you suffer from repeated nightmares or sudden awakenings at night? Do you wake too early in the morning? If the answer is 'yes' to any of these questions, you may need to keep a 'sleep diary' which will help you pinpoint the precise problem.

An example of a sleep diary is provided in Figure 4. Following this pattern, each morning write down how refreshed you feel, rating this feeling on a ten-point scale where 0 is 'extremely unrefreshed' and 10 is 'very refreshed'. You will also need to jot down the problem areas so that you can work out how to deal with them in order to improve the quality of your sleep.

There are some basic strategies we can use to improve our chances of sleeping well. You may already have discovered your own personal way of ensuring a refreshing night's sleep; some of the more common remedies are:

- try not to engage in any vigorous activity or tasks needing intense concentration in the hour before going to bed;
- have a relaxing warm bath or shower before bedtime;
- drink a glass of warm milk before going to bed (*not* coffee);
- try to avoid alcohol just before bedtime;
- listen to music or engage in a relaxing activity before bedtime;

- try to 'switch off the day's worries and stresses: you can think about them the next morning;
- use a relaxation exercise or tape (see section on 'Relaxation' below).

Relaxation

Taking time for relaxation and enjoyable activities is important to maintaining a sense of well-being. Finding some time every week simply to enjoy ourselves is necessary to allow us to unwind and recharge our batteries.

We all differ in what we find enjoyable. Meditation may be the best way to relax for some, while for others going to a movie may be an effective distraction. Others may enjoy going to the beach, gardening or fishing. Some people may prefer to engage in leisure activities for a short period in every day, while others prefer to save up their time so that they can enjoy themselves at more length once a week. Whatever your preference, it is important to set aside some time regularly, whether daily or weekly, to do something you enjoy.

In choosing relaxation activities, make sure they really are ones *you* enjoy, and that you are not participating in them just to please someone else. In the space below, list some of the relaxing activities that you enjoy. They may be things you haven't done for a while, or things you have often thought you would like to do one day, as well as things you already do sometimes.

Relaxing activities	How often do you do them?
1.	
2.	
3.	
4.	
5.	

Another method of relaxing is to use a technique known as *progressive muscle relaxation*. This exercise, if practiced regularly, will help to reduce muscle tension and other stress symptoms. The technique involves progressively tensing and relaxing the major muscle groups in the body while maintaining your breathing at a slow rate. The exercise needs to be practiced at least once a day in order to be effective. If you can find the time to do it twice a day, the benefits will be greater. Most people find that they notice positive effects after two to three weeks of regular practice. When you begin, find a convenient time of the day to ensure that you can perform the exercise regularly. The most suitable times usually are in the morning when you first wake up and just before retiring for the night. You can use the self-monitoring form on p. 80 to remind yourself to be regular in carrying out the exercise. There are extra forms at the end of the book.

There are several commercially available relaxation tapes that can help you to learn the technique. If you choose to use a tape, try practising without it as well, so that you can perform the exercises independently.

Once you have mastered this technique, try applying a mini-relaxation exercise in situations where you cannot carry out the full exercise. Even on a bus or a train, you can close your eyes, practice your slow breathing, mentally say 'relax', and gently tense and relax the muscles of either your hands or feet. With practice, this mini-relaxation exercise can be almost as effective as the full-scale method.

Review of Step 2

In Step 2 we have examined some of the ways in which you can improve your physical health and thereby reduce your vulnerability to stress. Now that you have read the chapter, try to answer the following questions about your current lifestyle and how you might improve it:

- Are you currently engaging in any regular exercise? If not, what type of exercise could you start doing on a regular basis?

- Is your diet adequate? Are you eating regular meals? Have you reduced your intake of coffee, tea and chocolate? Are you on a program to stop smoking? Are you ensuring that your alcohol consumption is reduced to safe levels?

- Are you experiencing difficulties in falling asleep or staying asleep? Are you waking too early? What can you do to improve your sleep?

- Are you allowing yourself enough time for relaxation and recreation? If not, how can you reorganize your schedule so that you can make sufficient time?
- When can you practice the progressive muscle relaxation exercises? How are you going to ensure that you practice them at least once and preferably twice a day?

Altering your lifestyle so that it becomes less stressful may take several weeks or even months. There may be several barriers to change. However, if you start with small changes to your lifestyle, then the larger changes may not seem so threatening or overwhelming. Make sure that you are not attempting to change too many aspects of your lifestyle too quickly, and that you accept that there may be interruptions and distractions. The important message is to treat any setbacks as temporary and to resume your program as soon as possible.

- Find a comfortable, quiet place to sit or lie down, and try to ensure that you will not be interrupted for about twenty minutes. It may be necessary to tell the people that live with you that you do not want to be disturbed, or organize time to be alone in a quiet room.
- Close your eyes and focus on your breathing, keeping it slow and even. Say the word 'relax' to yourself a few times as you breathe out.
- Tense your right foot, squeezing your toes together and pointing them downwards. Focus on that tension. Slowly release that tension as you breathe out, saying the word 'relax' to yourself.
- Now tense your right calf muscle and hold the tension for a while. Slowly release the tension as you breathe out.
- Progress through your body, working through the muscles of your right leg, left leg, buttocks, back, abdomen, chest, shoulders, left arm, left hand and fingers, right arm, right hand and fingers, neck, jaw, lips, eyes, and forehead, tensing and relaxing for each group of muscles in the same way.
- Scan through your body and make sure that most of the tension has been released. If some areas are still tense, spend extra time relaxing those muscles.
- Slowly open your eyes. Try to maintain that feeling of relaxation for the rest of the day; or, if it is evening, as you go to bed and prepare for sleep.

Figure 5. Progressive muscle relaxation: the technique

Daily self-monitoring form for muscle relaxation exercises

Effectiveness rated from 0 to 10 where 0 = not at all effective and 10 = very effective

	Monday	Tuesday	Wednesday	Thursday	Friday	Saturday	Sunday
✓ A.M.	☐ ☐	☐ ☐	☐ ☐	☐ ☐	☐ ☐	☐ ☐	☐ ☐
Effectiveness rating							
Comments							
✓ P.M.	☐ ☐	☐ ☐	☐ ☐	☐ ☐	☐ ☐	☐ ☐	☐ ☐
Effectiveness rating							
Comments							

Step 3

Controlling panic attacks

In Step 2, we considered ways of reducing your overall stress levels by making changes in your lifestyle. We discussed approaches to improving your physical health that could reduce your vulnerability to stress symptoms and panic attacks. Changing lifestyle can take time, so that you should continue with your program to improve your sleep, exercise, diet and relaxation patterns at the same time as you begin to practice specific exercises to combat symptoms of panic. Like any new skill, learning to control your panic attacks may take time, and you may need quite a lot of practice before you feel confident in using the techniques. Remember that achieving control over panic symptoms will help you to participate in activities that you may have been avoiding because of a fear of having panic attacks; this in turn may help your physical well-being and so start you on a 'benevolent' cycle away from stress and anxiety.

Step 3 deals with specific ways to control symptoms of panic. You may already be familiar with some of these techniques; others may be completely new to you. By practising these techniques regularly, you will equip yourself to prevent the debilitating symptoms of panic and to control minor symptoms of anxiety when they do occur.

Controlling overbreathing or hyperventilation

You may find yourself breathing faster for several reasons such as when you have a fever, during strenuous exercise or after you have experienced a sudden shock. In these situations an increased rate of respiration is a perfectly normal response. Some people, however, develop a habit of over-breathing, especially when they are stressed or worried. Overbreathing itself can trigger a panic attack, as discussed earlier. Once the panic attack starts, breathing becomes difficult or irregular and the 'hyperventilation – panic' cycle begins.

In Part One, Chapter 3, we discussed how hyperventilation causes unpleasant physical sensations by changing the balance of gases in the bloodstream. These effects can be reversed simply by slowing your breathing rate so that you increase the amount of carbon dioxide in the blood. By reversing the process of hyperventilation, you will find yourself feeling less aroused, less anxious and less likely to experience symptoms of panic.

We focus here on two ways of increasing the amount of carbon dioxide in the bloodstream in order to prevent a panic attack. You can use these techniques individually or in combination to control your panic attacks. Try both.

Slow breathing

This techniques may be used anywhere and takes only a few minutes. The aim of the exercise is to slow your breathing rate to about eight to ten breaths per minute when you feel anxious or panicky. If you practice the exercise regularly, and learn to keep your normal breathing rate at the correct level, you will be more able to control your breathing when you notice early symptoms of panic.

- Begin by focusing your attention on your breathing. Try not to control your breathing rate just yet, but concentrate on the sensation of breathing. If your mind wanders off to other things, gently redirect your attention back to your breathing.
- Practice 'abdominal' breathing. Place one hand over your stomach and gently expand the muscles in that region every time you breathe in. At the same time try to reduce movements in your chest and shoulders during breathing. If necessary, watch yourself in the mirror to ensure that your shoulders hardly move. This technique stops you from taking gasping, sharp breaths.
- Now, on your next breath in, hold your breath to the count of ten (for ten seconds). Do not take an excessively deep breath. If holding your breath to the count of ten is too difficult, try holding your breath to the count of eight.
- Now slowly exhale.
- Now breathe in to the slow count of three and then out to the slow count of three. Keep breathing in and out to the count of three, trying not to take overly deep breaths. Try pacing your breathing so

that it takes three seconds to inhale and three seconds to exhale.
- Continue breathing at this rate for at least one minute.
- If you still feel panicky, hold your breath for a further ten seconds and repeat the exercise. Continue practising the exercise until the sensations of panic subside.

If you practice this exercise regularly and frequently, five or six times a day, you will find that you can control your breathing at all times. Turn it into a secret 'game' you play on the bus, at traffic lights, or whenever you have an idle moment. With practice you will be able to use this exercise to control panicky sensations before they turn into full-blown panic attacks.

The paper bag technique

This method of controlling overbreathing increases the amount of carbon dioxide in the bloodstream simply by restricting the amount of oxygen that enters your lungs and increasing your intake of carbon dioxide as you breathe back in air you have already exhaled. (Don't worry: you are still absorbing ample amounts of oxygen!) The method does not involve as much practice as the slow breathing technique, but obviously is less easily used in public.

- When you feel panicky, place a small paper bag over your mouth and nose. Keep the bag firmly in place by holding it close to your face with your hands. Try not to allow any gaps where air can escape.

- Now breathe slowly and regularly into the bag. Keep breathing in and out into the bag until the panic attack begins to subside and your breathing becomes easy.
- A similar effect can be achieved by cupping your hands around your nose and mouth and breathing slowly.

To use this technique, you will need to carry a paper bag with you in your handbag or pocket. In public, the hand-cupping technique is more convenient. If you find a private place where you can use the paper bag, however, the technique will help you restore the balance of gases in your blood quickly and so help to control your anxiety.

Distraction techniques

Focusing your attention on your symptoms usually makes them worse and increases the severity of the panic attack. There are a number of techniques that can help you to take your mind off the sensations of panic. You probably have found some of your own already. Four that have been found particularly useful by panic sufferers are outlined here. Try them all to see which ones work best for you.

1. *The rubber band technique* Wear a rubber band loosely around your wrist. When you feel a panic attack

starting, stretch the rubber band out and let it snap back on to the inside of your wrist. Often the short, sharp sensation of pain will be enough to redirect your attention away from the beginning of panic symptoms. This can give you time to begin using some of the other techniques for controlling anxiety, such as the slow breathing technique. Sometimes the rubber band technique by itse If is enough to stop a panic attack from developing.

2. *Counting* Some people find that if they focus on counting objects in their environment, they can distract themselves from an imminent panic attack. You could count the number of red cars passing by on the road or the number of windows in a building. Or you could multiply numbers in your mind. There are several possible ways of distracting yourself using the counting technique.

3. *Visualizing* It can be relaxing to imagine yourself in a pleasant or enjoyable setting, away from the cares of daily life. When you begin to experience early signs of anxiety, try imagining a pleasant scene from your memory, or from a movie or book. For example, try visualizing a warm summer day at the beach, or a walk through a beautiful park. Think of a scene that is special for you alone, and try to make the details (sounds, sights, smells) as real as possible. Practicing the same scene over and over will help you slip more easily into the exercise when necessary.

4. *Intellectualizing* Another method of distraction is to 'intellectualize' the symptoms of panic. This

involves acknowledging the symptoms in an objective manner. For example, while feeling anxious you can note down all the symptoms and fears you experience and rate their severity. This technique suits some people who can step back from themselves and their anxieties to 'self-examine' and record their experiences. The panic attack becomes an external 'thing' that you can examine from a distance rather than an event that seems to be controlling you.

Simple, everyday activities like talking to a friend on the telephone, listening to the radio or watching television can also help to distract you from your panic sensations.

A package of coping techniques to deal with panic attacks

It is important to learn which techniques work best for you when you feel anxious so that you will be better prepared to face difficult situations, armed with the confidence of knowing how to combat *your* anxiety. Make a list of distraction techniques you have tried and consider how effective they were. Give them each a rating out of 10. This exercise may help you select more carefully which techniques to use in the future.

It may be helpful to write down all the techniques that help you to control your panic attacks, perhaps on a card which you can carry around in your purse or wallet. By doing this you will be able to remind yourself quickly about what to do whenever you feel anxious or panicky.

For example, you might write the following instructions on a small card:

- hold breath for ten seconds;
- do slow breathing exercise;
- focus attention on counting technique.

Or:

- snap rubber band on wrist;
- put paper bag over nose and mouth;
- breathe slowly;
- visualize peaceful scene.

Once you begin to feel the panic attack subsiding, try to remain where you are and to continue what you were doing, but at a slower pace. For example, if you have a panic attack in the shopping centre, try to stay there for a while after the attack has subsided even if you are only walking around slowly. Escaping from a situation because of a panic attack may make it difficult to go back to that situation later. Try to reward yourself for coping with the panic attack by treating yourself to something you like or by praising yourself for handling the event as well as you did.

Review of Step 3

Step 3 has described some important techniques for preventing and controlling panic attacks. With regular practice of these techniques, you will be better able to overcome symptoms of panic and to resume the activities that you may have been avoiding. Of course, there may still be times when you experience symptoms of anxiety despite practising these skills. The occasional panic attack or anxiety symptom is only to be expected during recovery from panic disorder. Try treating the recurrence of anxiety as a minor setback that allows you to practice your skills further. Keep repeating to yourself that you are on the path to recovery and that the occasional slip along the way does not mean that you are falling back to the beginning.

Review your progress in Step 3 by asking yourself the following questions:

- Are you managing to slow down your breathing rate?
- Are you practicing your chosen breathing exercise regularly?
- Which distraction techniques work best for you?
- Have you written down those helpful techniques on a card, using the card promptly when needed?
- Are you managing to remain in difficult situations at least until the anxiety begins to subside?

When you are able to answer 'yes' to all these questions, you are ready to progress to the next step. Step 4 examines thinking styles that may be contributing to anxiety and panic attacks.

Step 4

Changing unhelpful thinking styles

Most of us have experienced periods in our lives when we have been extremely worried – about our health, our families or our friends, our jobs, our finances or our futures. Worrying about things is normal and even useful, since it enables us to anticipate and solve problems. Excessive worry, however, can become a problem in itself and may prevent us from focusing on the positive aspects of our lives. If worry becomes intense and prolonged, we are likely to experience physical symptoms such as muscle tension, sweating, churning in the stomach, and dryness of the throat and mouth. In some people, increasing tension may trigger panic attacks. As we have already noted (Part One, Chapter 3), physical symptoms of anxiety in themselves often cause worry about health, creating fears of serious illness and hence increasing anxiety.

In Step 2, we saw how physical factors such as tiredness, low levels of fitness and poor health could worsen symptoms of stress and anxiety. We also discussed the mind-body link to demonstrate how lack of sleep, poor diet and other physical factors reduce our resistance to stress. In Step 3 we discussed how hyperventilation can trigger panic attacks and looked at some methods of coping with panic symptoms. In Step 4 we will explore how you can deal with worrisome thoughts or negative thinking styles that can make you more vulnerable to suffering from anxiety and panic attacks.

There are three stages in considering and managing negative thinking styles. The first stage is learning to identify your negative thoughts; the second stage is learning how to challenge them, and the third stage is changing them to more positive, constructive thoughts that will reduce unnecessary anxiety. This three-step process is summarized in Figure 6.

1 Recognizing your 'negative' thoughts

2 'Challenging' your negative thoughts

3 Substituting 'positive' or more helpful thoughts

Figure 6. Overcoming negative thinking

Identifying negative thinking

How we interpret experiences, situations and sensations influences the way we feel about them and hence our emotional states. For example, if you think that you are going to suffer from a panic attack in a shopping mall, you may find yourself becoming very nervous every time you go shopping. As mentioned in Part One of this book, this is called *anticipatory anxiety*. What this means is that, just by predicting anxiety, you increase the risk of a panic attack actually happening. When the attack occurs, it strengthens the belief that you always will have a panic attack in that situation, and you become convinced that anxiety is unavoidable and uncontrollable. In effect, you are giving yourself a negative message: 'I told you so!'

In this way our ideas, thoughts and beliefs can lead to unpleasant emotions like anxiety, anger or depression. Because these emotions are so unpleasant, we may begin to avoid those situations where we predict that these feelings are likely to occur. We are made upset not so much by *actual* places or events as by our *interpretations* and *expectations* of places or events.

Most situations can be interpreted in different ways. We may be in the habit of interpreting situations in a way which regularly creates feelings of anxiety and panic. By practising alternative (but realistic) interpretation of these situations, we can reduce our anxiety reactions.

Some examples of negative thoughts are:

'I know for sure that I will have a panic attack if I go into any department store.'

'I'm definitely going to faint and no one will help me.'

'This pain in my chest must be a heart attack. I am going to die.'

'Everyone will laugh at me if I have a panic attack here.'

'Once panic starts, nothing can stop it.'

Unhelpful thoughts such as these may arise repeatedly in certain situations. These 'automatic' thoughts appear suddenly in our mind, sometimes without our even being fully aware of them. It is as if we have a 'hidden commentator' in our minds predicting gloom and doom. This tendency to interpret situations negatively arises from many influences including our upbringing, the expectations of those around us and the impact of the society in which we live.

A particularly unhelpful aspect of these interpretations is that they are overgeneralizations. For example, after having a panic attack on a bus, you may assume that you will have similar attacks on all forms of transport. These ideas cause a vicious cycle: because we tend to avoid the situations that we predict will lead to anxiety and fear, we avoid testing out these overgeneralizations and so are never able to find out how unhelpful or untrue they really are. If you have stopped going to department stores, it is difficult to know whether you will still have panic attacks in that environment. This vicious cycle effectively locks the sufferer into a restricted life of fear.

Figure 7 shows two examples of negative thoughts and the situations in which they occur. Fill in the blank spaces with negative thoughts that you have had in difficult situations.

Examples of negative thinking styles

There are several types of negative or faulty thinking styles, all of which serve to increase anxiety levels or to make us feel despondent

Situation	Negative thought
Shopping in a department store	'I can't cope with this anxiety'
Appointment at the hairdresser	'What if I have a panic attack and can't get out quickly?'

Figure 7. Examples of negative thinking

or demoralized. Below are some examples of faulty thinking styles observed by Albert Ellis, a therapist specializing in methods of challenging negative attitudes. See if you recognize some of these thinking styles in yourself.

1. *Black-and-white thinking*, or seeing an event as either total success or total failure, with no gradations in between. For example: 'If I experience any anxiety symptoms when I go shopping, then I have failed completely in managing my anxiety.'
2. *Generalizing* from one situation to the next. If one situation does not work out well, then we may decide that all similar situations will also be difficult. For example: 'I was feeling panicky at the train station so I know I will be panicky whenever I try to take public transport' or 'I am still experiencing

some panicky symptoms when I go out so I know I can't go anywhere anymore.' We have already noted how overgeneralizing can set up a vicious cycle of avoidance.

3. *Magnifying unpleasant experiences or focusing only on negatives.* For example: 'I chaired a meeting and caught up with all my paperwork, but I then became panicky when I could not find a folder. The whole day was a complete write-off.'

4. *Overestimating failure and underestimating success.* For example: 'So what if I am a successful journalist? I am a worthless person because I suffer from anxiety symptoms' or 'Everyone thinks that I am a total failure because I have panic attacks.'

5. *Setting unrealistic expectations* and not allowing yourself to make any mistakes. For example: 'I am practicing all my anxiety management skills so I expect never to suffer from a panic attack again' or 'I expect to be cured by next week.'

6. *Taking responsibility for others' feelings.* For example: 'It's my fault that the party was a failure – it must be because I was anxious' or 'it's my fault that my anxiety symptoms make my family upset.'

7. *Mind-reading other people's thoughts* or assuming certain outcomes without checking the facts. For example: 'They think I am stupid because I suffer from panic attacks' or 'I know for sure that I will have a panic attack if I try to drive over the bridge.'

You may be using some of these negative thinking styles without being fully aware that you are doing so. Remember, these thoughts can become habitual, flashing through your mind quickly, upsetting you without your realizing exactly why.

Every time you become upset or anxious, even if only slightly, say to yourself 'STOP'. Then try to assess exactly what the train of thought was that led to that feeling. See if you can link the negative thoughts to anything that has happened or been said recently. Can you detect a particular pattern in your negative thinking?

Challenging negative thoughts

Having identified your negative thinking habits, your next step is to learn how to change those thoughts to more positive, appropriate ones. This involves critically examining those thoughts and considering how accurate they really are. There are three ways of challenging your negative thoughts:

1. *Questioning the evidence for the negative thought*
   You may need to examine the probability of a negative thought being true all of the time. For example, to challenge the thought 'I am sure to have a panic attack. if I go into the department store,' you may need to consider whether you *automatically* have panic attacks in *all* department stores. What evidence do you have that suggests that you will *definitely* have a panic attack in this situation? Recall the

times that you did *not* have an attack, or had only minor symptoms while shopping.

Another way of questioning the evidence for a negative thought is to check whether your expectations of yourself are unrealistic. Are you expecting yourself *never* to experience *any* symptoms of anxiety when you go shopping?

2. *Checking out other possibilities before jumping to a conclusion* Before deciding that your negative interpretation of yourself or of a situation is the only 'correct' one, consider alternative ways of interpreting the same situation. For example, if you experience sensations such as not feeling 'with it', slight dizziness, weakness or feeling hot, try to consider other possible causes: did you stand up too quickly after sitting for a long time? Were you feeling excited? Was the room overheated? Were there other factors (strenuous exercise, hot weather, tiredness, viral illness) that could have produced some of those sensations?

3. *Asking others for their interpretation of a situation* This can be a useful method, especially if there is someone who can provide an accurate account of a particular event. Close friends, work colleagues, spposes or relatives often can help you to see a situation from a different and possibly more realistic perspective.

Try challenging some of your own negative thoughts by completing the exercise set out in Figure 8. Look at the two examples in the figure. Now select three recent instances when you felt anxious. Identify the situations you were in.

Consider the negative thoughts you experienced on each occasion. Try challenging those thoughts using the strategies of 'questioning the evidence' and 'checking out other possibilities'. Do you notice that your anxiety level changes when you start challenging your negative thoughts?

Situation	Negative thought thought	Challenging and considering an alternative
Going to supermarket on a hot day and experiencing panic symptoms	'I'll never get better'	'It was hot and I was rushing. Next time I will take it slower, choose a less busy time and make sure to stop for a drink. I have already made some progress and if I continue to improve I will eventually get better.'
Visiting family and having a heated deated discussion; feeling dizzy and experiencing rapid heartbeats	'I'm going to have a heart attack'	'I have been through several medical investigations and there is nothing wrong with my heart. My symptoms improved as soon as we left. I must have become overexcited. I know that

		if I was having a heart attack, I would not be feeling better so quickly.'
_____ _____ _____ _____ _____	_____ _____ _____ _____ _____	_____ _____ _____ _____ _____

Figure 8. Challenging negative thoughts

Changing negative thoughts to positive thoughts

In the last two sections we considered how negative thoughts about ourselves and our ability to cope in different situations can lead to anxiety symptoms and panic attacks, and how the act of challenging these thoughts can reduce anxiety by making our excessive worries less 'believable'. The next stage in overcoming negative thoughts is to substitute more positive thoughts for the unpleasant, unhelpful ones.

Rather than thinking those gloomy or fearful thoughts that may result in anxiety symptoms, what would you like to be able to say to yourself instead? Most people would like to be able to say to themselves 'I can cope with this' or 'I'll be all right.' What sorts of encouraging thoughts would you like to say to yourself the next time you encounter a difficult situation? Look at the examples in Figure 9 and then add some of the things you would like to think in the situations that worry you.

Situation	Positive thought
Department store	'I can handle my anxiety'
Hairdresser	'I am going to enjoy having my hair cut'
_____	_____
_____	_____
_____	_____
_____	_____
_____	_____

Figure 9. Examples of positive thinking

Now try the three-step process for yourself. Think back to the last time you felt anxious or panicky and try to recall the kinds of negative thoughts that were going through your mind. First describe the situation.

Situation: _____

_____

Now write down any negative thoughts, either about yourself or about the situation, that you remember.

Negative thoughts: _____

_____

What can you say to yourself to challenge those negative thoughts? Try questioning the evidence for them, using the techniques discussed in the previous sections of Step 4. What could you say to yourself to make the negative thoughts less 'believable'?

Challenging thoughts: _____

_____

Now that you have challenged those negative thoughts, do you notice that your anxiety about the situation has decreased? Have you managed to make your negative thoughts less 'believable'? If you have, then the final stage is to substitute more positive, helpful thoughts about the same situation. What encouraging things could you say to yourself?

Positive thoughts: _____

_____

At first, this exercise may seem a little difficult. However, with practice you will find that you are better able to recognize and challenge negative thoughts and finally to substitute more helpful, positive thoughts about yourself and the activities you undertake. Use the monitoring form opposite to help you practice this technique further. (There are extra forms at the end of the book.)

Self-monitoring form for changing negative thoughts

Rate anxiety level from 0 to 10 where 0 = not at all anxious and 10 = extremely anxious

Day/date	Negative thought	Anxiety level	Challenging thought	Positive/appropriate thought

Further ways to help change negative thoughts

How many times have you thought to yourself that you can give others good advice about coping with stress but cannot solve similar problems of your own? You could try to 'advise' yourself on how to change your negative thoughts by treating yourself as a good friend whose problems you understand very well. What would you say to someone who is seeking your advice about anxiety and panic attacks?

Another technique is to imagine someone you know who always manages to look on the bright side of a difficult situation. How would this person interpret a situation that you find difficult? What sorts of positive, encouraging thoughts would this person think? Sometimes, just putting yourself in someone else's shoes can help you to look at a situation differently, especially if that person has a positive outlook on life.

You can also check your own thoughts about a situation with someone who is close to you and knows you fairly well. Develop the habit of discussing the way you see a situation with someone else if that situation makes you feel tense or anxious. Another person might immediately see the negative aspect of your perception when it is not obvious to you. This could help you practice 'thinking straight' by looking at alternative explanations for situations you find difficult. Try not to hold on to particular negative interpretations of yourself and of the situations you encounter. Instead, get into the habit of looking at a situation from different angles.

'Cue cards' can be a useful way to remind yourself of positive, encouraging thoughts. These are small cards that can be carried in your purse or wallet and read whenever you feel yourself slipping back into negative thinking styles. Write a single positive thought on each card and use as many cards as you need. Whenever you feel the need to remind yourself of positive thoughts, read through these cards. You can use them when out shopping, while using public transport, or in any other situation that may be difficult for you. With repeated practice, these positive thoughts will become 'second nature' to you and you may not need to use the cards any more.

Review of Step 4

By now you are better able to recognize your negative thoughts, and to challenge and change them to more positive, helpful thoughts. Remember that thinking styles are learned over time. Like any other habit, they take time and practice to change. Rewarding yourself for overcoming each negative thought can be a helpful way to break the habit of thinking negatively. Try to reward yourself whenever you 'think straight' and manage to overcome your anxiety.

Review your progress by answering the following questions:

- Can you identify some of your negative thoughts that may be leading to anxiety and panic?
- Are you being effective in challenging your negative thoughts?
- What positive or encouraging thoughts would you like to substitute for those negative thoughts?

- Have you developed a list of cue cards to use when you feel anxious?
- Are you using your cards regularly?

If you are able to answer 'yes' to the above questions, proceed to Step 5, which deals with your anxieties about the physical sensations of panic.

Step 5

Dealing with physical sensations

For many people who suffer from panic disorder, physical sensations that remind them of symptoms of panic may increase their worry and anxiety. If these health concerns are particularly severe or prolonged, they may in turn trigger panic attacks. In this way a vicious cycle is created in which physical symptoms trigger panic attacks and panic leads to a greater focus on physical sensations.

Have you noticed that certain changes in your bodily sensations (such as a rapid heartbeat while walking) make you concerned that you might be having a panic attack? If so, then you are among the many sufferers who have started to fear 'normal' physical sensations, mistaking them for signs of imminent panic.

Which physical sensations remind you of symptoms of panic? In the space below list the ones that you associate with feelings of anxiety and panic:

1. _____

2. _____

3. _____

4. _____

5. _____

What activities do you avoid because they are more likely to lead to these symptoms? Many people suffering from panic disorder avoid strenuous activity and regular exercise for this reason. For example, a swim might cause temporary shortness of breath. This lack of exercise can result in poor physical fitness and an increased vulnerability to stress. People suffering from panic disorder also tend to avoid confrontations with family members, friends or colleagues. Arguments and disagreements can produce high levels of emotional arousal, causing flushing of the face, shallow breathing, and a dry throat and mouth. These sensations are very similar to those experienced during a panic attack. To avoid these sensations, people suffering from panic disorder may find it easier to 'give in' or to agree with friends or members of their family too easily simply to keep the peace. Unassertive behavior can become a habit leading to other problems in your personal and social life, such as not standing up for yourself when necessary.

To break this chain of negative effects, it is important to recognize the activities or situations that you may be avoiding so as not to become too aroused. In the space below list some of the situations that you avoid for fear of triggering physical sensations that remind you of panic:

	Activity	Physical sensations
1.		
2.		
3.		
4.		
5.		

Learning not to be fearful of 'normal' physical sensations

Two methods are suggested here to help you overcome fears about 'normal' physical sensations that remind you of panic attacks. If you practice both, you should find that you become able to accept these feelings without anxiety.

Desensitization of exposure

The first technique involves allowing yourself to experience normal physical sensations of arousal while controlling your anxiety levels. It is difficult to remain anxious if you experience the same sensation repeatedly without suffering any negative effects. In Step 3 we discussed a breathing technique aimed at helping you to control your anxiety and panic attacks. The same technique can be used to help you overcome your fears of physical sensations.

Go back to your list of feared physical sensations. Can you think of ways to produce these sensations? Below is a list of suggested ways of experiencing those sensations that remind you of panic symptoms:

Physical sensations	How to produce this sensation
Rapid heart rate	Physical activity such as walking, slow jogging, walking up and down stairs, or doing push-ups or sit-ups
Sweating	Physical activity as listed above or walking about in hot weather, taking a hot bath, wearing warm clothes
Trembling or muscle weakness	Make a fist and squeeze hard: hold the tension in your hand for a few minutes and suddenly release it
Shortness of breath, panting	Exercise such as fast walking, slow jogging or swimming
Dizziness	Spin slowly around with your eyes open, or spin slowly on a swivel chair

For any of the sensations that are not produced by vigorous exercise, you can use the slow breathing technique described in Step 3 to control your anxiety levels. Slow breathing will be effective for controlling anxiety when you experience sensations of sweating, dizziness or muscle weakness. For the fears associated with rapid heart rate and shortness of breath, it is best to wait these out or to use the technique described in the next section to control your anxiety level.

You may also choose to use the muscle relaxation exercise described in Step 2 to reduce your overall level of arousal while you 'wait' out these sensations.

Use a gradual step-by-step approach that can be included in your exercise program. For example, choose a walk through a park where you know that there are benches at regular intervals. Gradually increase your pace of walking daily until you experience some sweating, increase in heart rate and in the rate of breathing. Then sit down at a bench and practice your minimuscle relaxation exercise, noting that the sensations fade gradually as you relax and rest.

Challenging catastrophic thoughts

In Step 4 of this book you learned how to identify, challenge and change the negative thoughts associated with anxiety and anxiety-provoking situations. Now you need to apply the same principles to overcoming your fears of physical sensations.

Physical sensation	Fearful thought
1. Rapid heart rate	'I'm having a heart attack'
2. Light-headedness	'I'm going crazy'; 'I'm going to faint'
3. _____	_____
4. _____	_____
5. _____	_____

Figure 10. Examples of catastrophic thinking

Physical sensation	Negative thought	Challenging thought	Positive thought
Sweating	'I'm going to have a panic attack'	It's a hot day, I must be hot. I'm only sweating because of the heat. I'll just remove my jacket'	This isn't a panic attack. My sweatiness will go away as I cool down. I can cope'

Figure 11. Challenging and changing negative thoughts

What are your thoughts when you experience these physical sensations? Figure 10 gives a couple of examples. Use the space in the figure to write down some of your own thoughts.

In Step 4 we saw how negative thoughts can be challenged by questioning the evidence, checking out other possibilities before jumping to conclusions, and asking others about their interpretations of the same situation. Use these techniques now to challenge your fears of physical sensations. What could you say to yourself to make these fears less believable? What would be a more sensible way of interpreting your physical sensations? The last stage of changing unhelpful thinking styles is to substitute more rational, encouraging thoughts. Try substituting positive, helpful thoughts in those situations where you previously tended to think negatively about physical sensations. Use the chart in Figure 11 to challenge and change your negative thoughts to more positive, helpful ones, using the example for guidance.

If you practice both these techniques regularly, you will become more effective in challenging the negative thoughts that tend to turn a normal physical sensation into a symptom of panic. Use both methods whenever you find that your anxiety is being triggered by physical sensations. You may need to produce some of those sensations repeatedly to become skilled in using a combination of slow breathing, relaxation and thought challenging to overcome your anxiety. Think up exercises that will help you get used to physical sensations and work out the combination of anxiety-reducing techniques that is most useful for you. Using 'cue cards', as described in Step 4, will help to remind you of the techniques to use when you begin to overreact to your physical sensations. Remember, these small cards can be carried around with you and used whenever you feel yourself slipping into anxiety.

Review of Step 5

In Step 5 we have considered ways of preventing fear of normal sensations associated with physical arousal. We have set out two techniques that can help overcome unnecessary anxiety associated with these sensations.

Review your progress by asking yourself the following questions:

- Have you made a list of the physical sansations that mimic panic?
- What methods can you use to produce those sensations?
- What are your negative thoughts associated with those sensations?
- Can you challenge those negative thoughts?
- Have you developed a list of positive, helpful thoughts to substitute for those negative thoughts?
- What other anxiety management techniques can you use to control the anxiety caused by mislabelling physical sensations?
- Have you written out cue cards to use when you start to react to your physical sensations?
- Are you using your cards regularly?

If you can answer 'yes' to all these questions, you are ready to start putting all the skills into practice. When you feel confident in applying these skills, you are ready to move on to Step 6, which deals with overcoming anxiety and agoraphobia in difficult situations.

Step 6

Overcoming agoraphobia and troubleshooting problem areas

By now you should be familiar with a number of techniques to control your anxiety symptoms. These skills will help you to return gradually to those activities that you may have been avoiding. As we have already seen, some people avoid or retreat from situations in which they become anxious so that they participate less and less in activities that they previously enjoyed. For example, if you fear driving you may avoid visiting friends, going shopping or looking for a job. In this way, a fear of driving can lead to major life problems like losing touch with friends, relying on family members for transport, or financial hardship. Although avoidance or withdrawal from stressful situations may be one way of reducing your anxiety in the short term, it always leads to other difficulties which greatly affect your lifestyle. Other ways of coping are possible, as you will have learned from working through this program.

The principles of gradual exposure

As discussed in Part One, Chapter 4, gradual exposure or systematic desensitization is an effective technique for overcoming fears or phobias of situations that are not really dangerous. Repeated exposure uncouples the 'fight or flight' response from the previously feared situation.

Several principles should be kept in mind when applying gradual exposure techniques:

1. It is important to work out and write down a hierarchy of feared places and situations, ranking them according to the level of anxiety that they provoke.
2. It is best to work through the list from least to most feared situations in a systematic way. It may be necessary to break down each task into a series of smaller ones, so that you overcome the fear step by step. It may be necessary to repeat the first step several times before your anxiety level falls enough to proceed to the next step. It is also best if you remain at your destination long enough for your anxiety to fall to comfortable levels before returning.
3. Don't try to rush up the scale of feared situations. It is important to progress at the rate which is right for you as an individual, so that wherever you are on the scale the level of anxiety you feel is never more than moderate and therefore is always manageable. It is better to progress slowly and steadily than to try to take bigger steps than you can manage and then feel discouraged by setbacks.

4. A number of tactics can be used to make exposure easier in the early stages of the exposure program. Select the most useful techniques from the anxiety management strategies you have learned. Not all will be useful in every situation, so try to plan ahead, noting which are likely to be the most useful for each situation.

5. A trusted companion such as a close friend or family member may be very helpful in the early stages of the exposure exercises. It is important, though, that the companion fully understands the purpose of the exercises and agrees to withdraw gradually during the program to allow you to develop full independence in approaching previously feared situations. It is critical that both sides of the partnership accept this and are open about it, as the companion may expect quicker progress than is possible, or you may be tempted to 'hold on' to the security provided by the companion for too long.

6. The most important principle is to remember that you are trying to work systematically. This means being committed to the program as a priority in your life, approaching the tasks one step at a time, practicing the exercises regularly, and being willing to take one step back if you have a setback. If you practice the exercises haphazardly, or give up for days at a time because you had a 'bad' outing, then progress will be much slower. Using the monitoring forms and plotting your progress week by week helps you to monitor your improvement and to see

that even if small setbacks occur, they do not necessarily mean that you are not making headway overall.

Making a ranked list of stressful situations

Drawing up a list of anxiety-provoking situations is the first step in overcoming the fear of them. Once you have done this you will be able to see more clearly the kinds of situations that lead to anxiety, as we discovered in Step 1. Remember that this list is specific to you: what you find distressing may not be so distressing to someone else. Listing these situations also will help you to focus on when and how to use your newly learned anxiety management skills. Remember, it is best to practice your stress management skills on 'easier' or 'less stressful' situations first. List the situations that are stressful to you on the form opposite and, in the space provided, rate the level of anxiety associated with each situation from 0 to 10, where 0 = no anxiety and 10 = highest level of anxiety. Examples may include:

- being alone at home;
- walking down the road;
- visiting the supermarket;
- driving over a bridge in heavy traffic;
- telling the kids to clean up their room.

You can then use this form to record the progress you make in reducing the 'anxiety ratings' of the various situations.

List of anxiety-provoking situations

Situation	Rating (0–10) (0 = no anxiety, 10 = highest level of anxiety)	Change in rating	
		Week 1	Week 2
1.			
2.			
3.			
4.			
5.			
6.			
7.			
8.			
9.			
10.			

Catching a bus: an example of gradual exposure

People with agoraphobia often have difficulty catching a bus, even though they were once quite able to do so. This offers a simple example of how gradual exposure can be carried out. Catching a bus may rate 4–5 on your list in terms of the level of anxiety it causes, so it is not too difficult a task to start with. You may decide that it is best to break the task down into three

segments: walking to the bus stop, catching the bus for one stop; and then catching the bus over the bridge to the shopping centre. It might be best to try stage 1 over three or four days, at first with the help of a companion. The first day, the companion accompanies you to the bus stop and you sit together in the bus shelter, waiting for your anxiety to diminish. (You may find it useful to practice your mini-relaxation exercise, as described in Step 2, while you are there.) You then return home together. The next day, you may repeat the same exercise, noting the decrease in your anxiety. The following day, your companion might follow you at fifty paces, then join you at the bus stop. Within a few days, you may find that you can walk to the bus stop and back on your own. The procedure is then repeated for catching the bus one stop, beginning with your companion accompanying you, then sitting a few rows behind you, and then seeing you off at the bus stop and meeting you at the next stop. In this gradual way, you can progress to catching the bus on your own and taking it to the shops. Of course, with modifications, the same sequence can be applied to driving a car, catching a train, walking to a shopping mall or going out to a restaurant.

Remember, learning to cope with anxiety is a gradual process that requires practice. If possible, start practicing your anxiety-controlling techniques in less distressing situations. Once you become more confident in applying these skills, you can apply them to more difficult situations.

Applying anxiety management techniques

In the following sections we will examine how to combine stress management skills to work through more complex situations that cause anxiety. Remember, there is no single set of steps that applies equally well for everyone, and each person must work at his or her own pace. You will need to discover the combination of techniques that is most helpful in managing your own stress levels effectively, and a comfortable pace to proceed at.

Often a combination of techniques that works on your physical as well as your psychological state is most effective in overcoming stress and anxiety. In Step 2, we discussed looking after your physical well-being by exercising, maintaining a good diet, and ensuring that you have enough sleep. We also discussed muscle relaxation exercises as an effective method for reducing tension. In Step 3, we considered various ways to help you control panic attacks, such as slow breathing and distraction techniques. Step 4 examined how to change negative thinking styles that can lead to symptoms of anxiety and to loss of confidence. These techniques can now be used individually or in combination to control your anxiety in a wide range of situations.

The next two sections look at how you might apply the skills you have learnt in two situations many panic sufferers find stressful: going to the supermarket and visiting the dentist.

The supermarket

Let us imagine that going to the supermarket rates 6 on your list of stressful situations. You may want to start the day by doing a brief muscle relaxation exercise before you leave the house. You may also need to use the slow breathing technique in the car park outside the supermarket to ensure that you are feeling calm and relaxed. You may then need to challenge your negative thoughts associated with supermarket shopping. Writing them down before you leave home may make this task a little easier. For example:

'I will have a terrible panic attack and lose control'
'I will look so anxious that other people will think
I am crazy'

These negative thoughts can be challenged in a number of ways:

'I do not always have panic attacks in supermarkets,
and even if I did get panicky, I know how to control my
symptoms'

> *'I have never lost control or started screaming when I go to the supermarket, and it is unlikely that I will do so now'*
>
> *'I look anxious, it is unlikely people will take special notice of me. Even if they do notice me looking anxious, they will not automatically think I am crazy. Lots of people look stressed in the supermarket'*

Finally, try substituting more positive, encouraging thoughts that will reduce your anxiety about going to the supermarket.

> *'I can cope with this'*
>
> *'I know how to keep my anxiety under control'*
>
> *'It will be over soon'*

If you have made up 'cue' cards to remind yourself of how to challenge your negative thoughts, you may want to look at them before going into the supermarket. Once inside, keep your breathing slow and even. Try pacing yourself so that you do not rush through the supermarket feeling overwhelmed and frantic. If you do get anxious, simply stop and focus on slowing your breathing while reading your 'cue' cards that help to challenge negative thoughts. While waiting at the checkout you might use distraction techniques like counting or visualization.

Finally, when you have completed your supermarket shopping, reward yourself with a small treat for having coped with the situation.

The dentist

Another commonly feared situation is going to the dentist for a check-up, a task which you may have rated 6. You could start preparing for this situation by making sure that you have a good night's sleep. Before leaving the house, practice your muscle relaxation exercise. Give yourself plenty of time to reach the dentist's surgery so that you do not feel rushed or flustered.

As with going to the supermarket, you may need to examine your negative thoughts before the visit. Write down some of your negative thoughts about going to the dentist. Your list may look something like this:

'I will scream or lose control when the dentist examines me'
'I will be so anxious that I may faint and the dentist will think I'm crazy'

Remember, the next step in modifying these negative thoughts is to begin to challenge them. You may want to start questioning your negative thoughts as follows:

'I have never screamed or lost control when I have gone to the dentist in the past and it is unlikely that I will do so now'
'I have never fainted at the dentist's surgery and it is unlikely that I will faint now. If I do feel faint, I can tell the dentist and she will give me time to recover'
'The dentist sees many patients who are anxious and it is unlikely that she thinks they are all crazy'

The last step is to substitute more positive thoughts that will help you to control your anxiety about going to the dentist:

> *'Even though it is uncomfortable visiting the dentist, it only last for half an hour. I can manage that'*
> *'I have ways of controlling my anxiety symptoms'*
> *'I can cope with going to the dentist. I am prepared for this visit'*

In the dentist's waiting room, scan through your body to detect any muscle tension. Ask yourself whether your body feels rigid or stiff. Carry out a quick muscle relaxation exercise by focusing on those areas that feel especially tense and then relaxing them. As you breathe out, say the word 'RELAX' to yourself. Do this a few times until you begin to feel those muscles actually relaxing and the tension reducing. Focus on your breathing, remembering to keep your rhythm slow and even. If you feel anxious, use your breathing control technique until you start to feel yourself relax. Try to maintain a feeling of calmness for as long as possible.

Mention to the dentist that you feel anxious and that you may need a little time between procedures to regain your equilibrium. Also, ask the dentist to explain each procedure to you and say how long it will take. Most dentists will agree beforehand to stop a procedure if you lift your hand up to signal the need for a break.

When the visit is over, reward yourself with a small treat for having coped with your anxiety.

Trouble-shooting problem areas

Some situations trigger panic in a high proportion of people with panic disorder, especially those who also suffer from agoraphobia. In addition, there are individual anxieties that are specific to each person. Some of these personal triggers may be obvious and immediate, such as problems at work, at home, or in a relationship. Other problems may be more complex and have their roots in earlier experience. Dealing with such deeper problems is beyond the scope of this book. If you believe that you need help in that area, you would be best advised to seek counselling.

All of us have to deal with problems every day. The way in which we go about tackling these problems varies from person to person and from one situation to the next, and there is no 'best' way of solving problems; nevertheless, some ways of solving problems are better than others, especially in the long run.

Not dealing with problems as they arise can lead to feelings of helplessness and frustration, and may eventually lead to a worsening of panic symptoms. Some common but ineffective ways of coping with problems are:

- ignoring them, hoping that they will go away or that they will magically 'sort themselves out';
- relying on someone else to come up with a solution;
- worrying repeatedly about what has caused the problem rather than thinking of any possible solutions;

- relying on fate or luck to sort things out;
- becoming too distressed to deal with the problem.

If you find yourself resorting to any of these 'methods', you may be keeping yourself in a stressed state for longer than is necessary.

A more effective way of dealing with problems is to try to solve them yourself in a step-by-step way. An example of structured problem-solving follows.

Step 1: Define the problem
First, try to define what the problem area is. Be as specific as you can: this makes it easier to think of possible and appropriate solutions. For example:

I get anxious whenever I argue with my daughter about her excessive use of the telephone.

Once you have thought about what the problem is, write down as many solutions to this problem as you can think of. Be as imaginative or outrageous as you like.

Look through your list of solutions and rate each solution from -10 to +10, where -10 indicates a very poor solution and +10 indicates an extremely good solution. A middle rating of 0 indicates a solution with equal advantages and disadvantages.

Step 2: Define solutions	*Rating*
1. Leave the house whenever my daughter uses the telephone	-9

2. Disconnect the telephone   -5
3. Make her pay for her use of the telephone
   if it exceeds 'normal' usage   +7
4. Consider what types of negative thoughts
   may be contributing to my anxiety about her
   use of the telephone   +8
5. Install a separate extension for her to use in
   her room   +4

Now look through your list once again and decide which is the best solution to that particular problem. You may decide that there is more than one solution, or that a combination of solutions will work best. Write down your chosen solution or solutions to this problem.

Step 3: Best solution or combination of solutions
   1. Install another telephone and make her pay for
      her own telephone calls
   2. Examine my attitude about her use of the tele-
      phone and try to challenge any irrational thoughts
      that are causing unnecessary distress

Now consider how you will implement your solution to this problem. What is the best time to carry out your plan? Does the solution involve particular people or apply to certain places?

Step 4: How and when will you implement this solution?
Wait for the weekend when we are both at ease and

> then talk to my daughter in her room about this problem and the solutions I think would be best.

Finally, once you have tried a particular solution, it is important to review your efforts. How well did you manage to discuss this solution? Was it effective? If not, how can you modify it? Mark your solutions on a simple scale.

Step 5: Review your efforts

Easy to carry out this solution	Neither easy nor difficult to carry out	Impossible to carry out
Outcome very effective	Outcome neither effective nor ineffective	Outcome very ineffective

Effective problem-solving can prevent small problems from growing into major sources of stress which could make your panic symptoms worse. Try practicing this exercise on important problems you can identify in your life.

Review of Step 6

This step has involved your considering various combinations of techniques that work for you in different situations. Relaxation exercises beforehand and use of the breathing exercise may help to settle yourself in at the dentist's surgery. Challenging and substituting negative thoughts, and practicing slow breathing, may be useful in the supermarket. The most important thing is to identify and use the techniques that work best for you.

- We have seen, too, that another useful way of preparing for a situation is by practicing it in your mind, challenging the negative thoughts that can arise and imagining the stressful situation while you use your coping strategies to control your anxiety. In this way you can proceed through the imagined situation step by step and plan ahead which anxiety management strategies you will use at each point. When you have successfully practiced coping with a particular situation in your mind, you can try it out in 'real life'.

- Don't forget to reward yourself when you succeed at reducing your anxiety. You can go back to your original list and rerate each item as you lessen the worry it causes you. As you overcome your anxiety in a range of situations, your ratings will start to decrease to more manageable levels.

- Remember to work through your list of stressful situations slowly. Do not move on to the harder items until you feel some degree of confidence in completing the easier tasks. Keep practicing your coping skills regularly, as it is easy to become disorganized or confused when you are anxious. Try to use the structured problem-solving technique described above to help overcome some of your sources of stress.

- Once again, remember that effective stress management takes time and practice. Don't be discouraged if your anxiety remains high even after practicing all these skills. Be patient and learn from your experiences, even the ones that may not turn out exactly the way you want them to. Remember, it is virtually impossible to remain anxious if you expose yourself repeatedly to a situation that is not really dangerous.

Preventing setbacks

The six-step program described in Part Two focuses on various ways of coping with stress and panic attacks. Regular practice will make the techniques progressively easier to use; yet sometimes, despite all your efforts, it may seem as if you are going backwards rather than continuing to improve. It is easy to become demoralized by such setbacks, especially when they occur after you have been making progress for some time. This last section of the book considers ways of preventing these setbacks and overcoming them if they occur.

Understanding the pattern of recovery

Recovery from panic disorder and agoraphobia often follows a fluctuating course, and at times it may seem that you have reached a plateau or even that your anxiety has worsened. This pattern is part of the 'normal' recovery process, which can be depicted on a 'recovery graph' (see Figure 12). From this graph you can see that over a period of time, your symptoms tend to improve; however, there may be

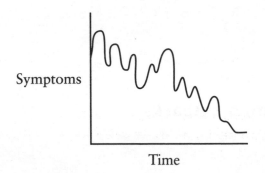

Figure 12. The normal pattern of recovery from panic disorder and agoraphobia

days, or even weeks, when your symptoms may flare up, just as there also may be times when symptoms improve rapidly, even more than expected. The important point to remember here is that despite fluctuations in the intensity and/or frequency of symptoms, if you practice your techniques, the level of anxiety will gradually follow a downward course and symptoms will diminish or disappear completely.

What is relapse?

Relapse is a more serious setback or recurrence of panic disorder. In other words, the symptoms that you managed to overcome or control may start to reappear for a variety of reasons. As a first step, it is important to distinguish 'relapse' from the normal recovery process which tends to have 'ups' and 'downs' over time. Answering the questions

	Yes	No
1. Are you experiencing full-blown panic attacks?	☐	☐
2. Have your symptoms returned at the same intensity as when they first occurred?	☐	☐
3. Are the symptoms increasingly interfering with your usual daily routine?	☐	☐
4. Has the frequency of these symptoms increased to the same level as when you first started experiencing panic attacks?	☐	☐

Figure 13. Checklist for relapse

shown in Figure 13 may help you to check whether you are experiencing a relapse of your symptoms. If you answer 'yes' to any of these questions, you may be experiencing an early stage of relapse and you may need to consider systematic ways of preventing the symptoms from worsening. In the following sections we examine ways of preventing setbacks from developing into a fullblown relapse.

Why do people relapse?

Usually, a combination of factors leads to relapse. This can include the recurrence of external stresses, difficulty coping with these problems, and insufficient or irregular practice of stress management techniques. Also, people who have suffered from panic disorder may continue to have trouble 'labelling' normal anxiety correctly, even after they have recovered, and so may mistake normal levels of stress (e.g. before an examination or a public speech) as signs of relapse. The worry about symptoms returning may itself provoke the recurrence of panic.

External stress is more likely to lead to a return of panic under certain conditions. You may be particularly vulnerable to stress because of lack of sleep, poor diet or physical illness. Low self-esteem and lack of confidence also may increase your vulnerability to anxiety symptoms. You may have given up practicing your anxiety-reducing techniques too early, or stopped taking your prescribed anti-anxiety medication too soon: suddenly ceasing medication can leave you vulnerable to anxiety symptoms. On the other hand, if your symptoms have changed in character, or you have any doubt about what is wrong, you should visit your doctor for a thorough reassessment.

Preventing relapse

There are many strategies that you can use to prevent relapse if you begin to feel stressed. Look back at the questions in Figure 13 earlier in this chapter. If you answered 'yes' to any of them you may find it useful to consider the following questions too, which may help to pinpoint ways of preventing yourself from relapsing.

Are there new stresses in your life, or are you becoming overly sensitive to minor anxiety symptoms leading you to worry unnecessarily?

You may need to refer back to Step 1in this program in order to refresh your memory about anxiety symptoms and sources of stress. Try to list the factors that may have contributed to your increased anxiety symptoms. Are any of the stresses similar to the ones you listed in Step 1, or are there new stresses that are adding to your worries?

Are you attempting to overcome your anxiety or avoidance of situations too quickly?

If you suddenly experience a full-blown panic attack after weeks or months of minimal anxiety symptoms, it may be an indications. that you are attempting too much too soon or without adequate preparation. If you have been trying concentratedly to overcome your avoidance of difficult situations, you may be pushing yourself a little too hard. Perhaps you need to rethink how much preparation you need before undertaking more difficult situations.

If you are becoming anxious about a new life challenge or change (e.g. a new job) assess the situation carefully before plunging into it. Use the techniques you have learnt to help you cope with the heightened tension that may be provoked by considering these options. If you do not feel ready for a particular challenge, do not force yourself to undertake it unless it is essential. The timing of new undertakings can be critical. If you do embark on a new venture, make sure that the rest of your lifestyle and stress management program are not disrupted.

Are you still maintaining a healthy lifestyle?

It is easy to forget about those lifestyle factors that may be affecting your anxiety levels, especially if you have had a long panic-free period. Re-examine your lifestyle, checking that you are eating a healthy diet, taking regular exercise and limiting your intake of stimulants like tea, coffee and cigarettes. Remember, an increase in alcohol intake may lower your threshold of panic.

Resume your relaxation exercises and slow breathing techniques if you have stopped doing them, and keep them up even when you do not feel especially anxious. All these techniques take time to master, and lack of practice can result in some loss of skills. You will be less able to control your anxiety if your stress management skills are rusty.

Have you suddenly stopped taking your prescribed medication, or been varying the dose?

Suddenly ceasing medication or changing the dose can lead to a resurgence of anxiety symptoms and panic attacks. Even if you feel a great improvement, it is best to keep taking your medication as prescribed until both you and your doctor decide to reduce the dosage. If your doctor has changed your medication and you are now experiencing increased anxiety or panic attacks, consult your doctor to try to work out whether these symptoms are likely to pass quickly or whether you need to return to the original dose.

Are you lapsing into unhelpful ways of thinking?
Remember to use the thinking exercises outlined in Step 4 to maintain a positive frame of mind. Challenge and re-evaluate any negative interpretations of events, your feelings and your physical sensations. Reinstitute your systematic program of substituting positive thoughts for any negative ones you have detected. Poor self-esteem and lack of confidence are directly related to negative thoughts, and vice versa. Remember to reward yourself for coping with your anxiety symptoms and to acknowledge your successes.

By systematically working through these questions, you will be better able to prevent yourself from slipping backwards. Go back to the exercises you learnt in Steps 1–6 to refresh your memory of how to overcome anxiety symptoms and panic attacks. If panic attacks continue, it may be useful to discuss the situation with your family doctor and perhaps seek referral to a mental health professional who specializes in the treatment of panic disorder. Remember that setbacks need not mean a return to your previous levels of anxiety symptoms. If you apply your techniques energetically to deal with temporary setbacks, you usually can put yourself back on the road to recovery very quickly.

A note on depression

For many people, depression and anxiety go hand in hand. For most people suffering from panic disorder, depressive feelings are fleeting or relatively minor: these people are able to sustain the energy and motivation to continue working on overcoming panic attacks and agoraphobia. For others, however, depression may become overwhelming. When this happens, it is necessary to seek professional help.

For minor bouts of depression, lasting a few hours or days, a self-help approach can be effective. An initial step is to write down what stresses may be contributing to the depression and then take a step-by-step approach to solving the immediate problems that you face. A further strategy may be to use distraction techniques (see Step 3) to focus your mind on pleasurable, non-stressful activities. This is especially effective if the cause of the depression cannot easily be eliminated. It may also be useful to examine whether negative thoughts or attitudes are contributing to depressive feelings. Learning to challenge these thoughts (see Step 4) is a useful skill that could be developed through further reading on the topic of depression.

If these techniques do not help to alleviate depression, or you are feeling hopeless or desperate, do seek professional help. Antidepressant medication together with regular counselling sessions may be required to overcome the depressive episode. In the unusual instance of depression being very severe, a period in hospital may be necessary, especially if the depression is so bad as to raise the risk of self-neglect or self-harm.

The recommended steps in dealing with depression are summarized in Figure 14.

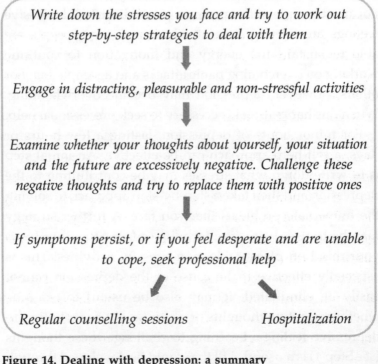

Write down the stresses you face and try to work out step-by-step strategies to deal with them

Engage in distracting, pleasurable and non-stressful activities

Examine whether your thoughts about yourself, your situation and the future are excessively negative. Challenge these negative thoughts and try to replace them with positive ones

If symptoms persist, or if you feel desperate and are unable to cope, seek professional help

Regular counselling sessions　　　*Hospitalization*

Figure 14. Dealing with depression: a summary

A final note

Now that you have worked through this self-help book, you are in a better position to take charge of your panic attacks and to participate fully again in all the activities you have avoided. Reread the book slowly if you feel yourself slipping back to the old lifestyle or thinking patterns that could increase the risk of panic attacks recurring.

If you find it difficult to maintain your motivation, you could consider joining a support group. For many people suffering from anxiety disorders, meeting other people who suffer from the same problems can be extremely helpful. To find out more about support groups, contact your family doctor or local mental health service. Attending a support group may be particularly beneficial if you suffer from panic disorder with agoraphobia.

Finally, remember that your experience of anxiety, although painful, has taught you valuable lessons about the impact of stress on your health and about the need to monitor and deal with stress when it occurs.

Useful books

There are a number of other books that you may find useful in understanding panic disorder and agoraphobia. Some of these take a broad-based approach to dealing with stress in general. The more reading you do, the greater the likelihood of picking up some useful skills for coping with panic attacks and agoraphobia. On the other hand, as in your use of this book, you need to be selective and critical in deciding which techniques work best for you.

The following titles may be helpful.

Dr Lee Baer, *Getting Control*, London, Little Brown, 1996.
Dancing with Fear, London, Jason Aronson, 1996.
Mark Greener, *The Which? Guide to Managing Stress*, London, Which? Books, 1996.
Gerlad L. Klerman *et al.* (eds), *Panic Anxiety and Its Treatments: Report of the World Psychiatric Association Presidential Educational Task Force*, New York, American Psychiatric Association, 1993.
Professor Isaac Marks, *Living with Fear*, New York, McGraw-Hill, 1978.

Joy Melville, *Phobias and Obsessions*, London, Macdonald Optima, rev. ed. 1991.

Reneau Z. Peurifoy, *Anxiety, Phobias and Panic: Taking charge and conquering fear*, New York, Warner Books, 1995.

Stanley Rachman and Padmal de Silva, *Panic Disorders: The Facts*, Oxford, Oxford University Publishing, 1996.

Shirley Swede, *Panic Attack Recover Book*, New York, New American Library-Dutton, 1989.

Robert E. Thayer, *The Origin of Everyday Moods: Managing energy, tension and stress*, Oxford University Publishing, 1996.

Shirley Trickett, *Coping with Anxiety and Depression*, London, Sheldon Press, 1989.

Useful addresses

United Kingdom
British Association for Behavioural and Cognitive Therapies
Victoria Buildings, 9–13 Silver Street
Bury
BL9 0EU
Tel.: 0161 7974484
Fax: 0161 7972670
Email: babcp@babcp.com
www.babcp.com

British Association for Counselling and Psychotherapy
BACP House, 15 St John's Business Park
Lutterworth, Leicestershire
LE17 4HB
Tel.: 0870 443 5252
Email: bacp@bacp.co.uk
www.bacp.co.uk

First Steps to Freedom
22 Randall Road
Kenilworth
Warwickshire CV8 1JY
Helpline: 01926 851608

Institute for Neuro-Physiological Psychology
Warwick House
4 Stanley Place
Chester CH1 2LU
Tel.: 01244 311414

Lifeskills
Bowman House
6 Billetfield
Taunton
Somerset TA1 3NN
(No telephone number available)

MIND: The National Association for Mental Health
Granta House
15–19 Broadway
Stratford
London E15 4BQ
Tel.:0181 519 2122 (can also give you details of local tranquil-
lizer withdrawal support groups)

No Panic
93 Brands Farm Way
Randlay
Telford
Helpline: 01952 590545

Open Door Association
447 Pensby Road
Heswall
Wirral
Merseyside LR 9PQ
(No telephone number available)

Phobic Action
Hornbeam House
Claybury Grounds
Woodford Creen
Essex IG8 8PR
(No telephone number available)

Phobics Society (a self-help network)
4 Cheltenham Road
Chorlton cum Hardy
Manchester M21 9QN
Tel.: 0161 881 1937

Relaxation for Living (courses and information to combat stress)
Dunesk, 29 Burwood Park Road
Walton-on-Thames
Surrey KT12 5LH
Tel.: 01932 227826

Triumph Over Phobia
(TOP UK)
PO Box 1831
Bath BA1 3YX
(No telephone number available)

United States

American Mental Health Foundation
2 East 86th Street
New York
NY 1008
(Written enquiries only)

Association for the Advancement of Behavior therapy
305 7th Avenue
New York
NY 10001
Tel.: 212 647 1890

The Behavior Therapy Center of New York
115 East 87th Street
New York
NY 10028
Tel.: 212 410 6500

Behavior Therapy Institute
San Francisco
Tel.: 415 989 2140

Behavioral Psychotherapy Center
23 Old Mamaroneck Road
White Plains
NY 10605
Tel.: 914 761 4080

Institute for Behavior Therapy
137 East 36th Street
New York
NY 10016
Tel.: 212 686 8778

Long Island Jewish Hospital at Hillside Phobia Clinic
New Hyde Park
NY 11040
Tel.: 718 470 7000 (Hospital number)

Institutes for Neuro-Physiological Psychology:
Dr Larry J. Beuret MD
48u Emerson, Suite 209
Palatine
IL 60067
Tel.: 847 303 1800
and
Mrs Victoria Hutton
6535 North Shore Way
Newmarket
Maryland 21774
Tel.: 301 607 6752

White Plains Hospital Center
Anxiety and Phobia Clinic
Davis Ave., at Post Road
White Plains
NY 10601
Clinic tel.: 914 681 0600
(Mon, Wed, Fri only, 9.00 a.m.–4.00 p.m.

Australia and New Zealand

Triumph Over Phobia
TOP NSW
PO BOX 213
Rockdale
New South Wales 2216
Australia

Institutes for Neuro-Physiological Research:
Dr Mary Lou Sheil
80 Alexandra Street
Hunters Hill 2110
Sydney, Australia
Tel.: 298 796 596
and
Heather Jones
501 North Willowport Road
Hastins
New Zealand
(No telephone number available)

Extra monitoring sheets

Self-monitoring from for changing negative thoughts

Rate anxiety level from 0 to 10 where 0 = not at all anxious and 10 = extremely anxious

Day/date	Negative thought	Anxiety level	Challenging thought	Positive/appropriate thought

Self-monitoring fram for changing negative thoughts

Rate anxiety level from 0 to 10 where 0 = not at all anxious and 10 = extremely anxious

Day/date	Negative thought	Anxiety level	Challenging thought	Positive/appropriate thought

Self-monitoring from for changing negative thoughts

Rate anxiety level from 0 to 10 where 0 = not at all anxious and 10 = extremely anxious

Day/date	Negative thought	Anxiety level	Challenging thought	Positive/appropriate thought

Self-monitoring from for changing negative thoughts

Rate anxiety level from 0 to 10 where 0 = not at all anxious and 10 = extremely anxious

Day/date	Negative thought	Anxiety level	Challenging thought	Positive/appropriate thought

Self-monitoring from for changing negative thoughts

Rate anxiety level from 0 to 10 where 0 = not at all anxious and 10 = extremely anxious

Day/date	Negative thought	Anxiety level	Challenging thought	Positive/appropriate thought

Self-monitoring from for changing negative thoughts

Rate anxiety level from 0 to 10 where 0 = not at all anxious and 10 = extremely anxious

Day/date	Negative thought	Anxiety level	Challenging thought	Positive/appropriate thought

Monitoring form for panic attacks

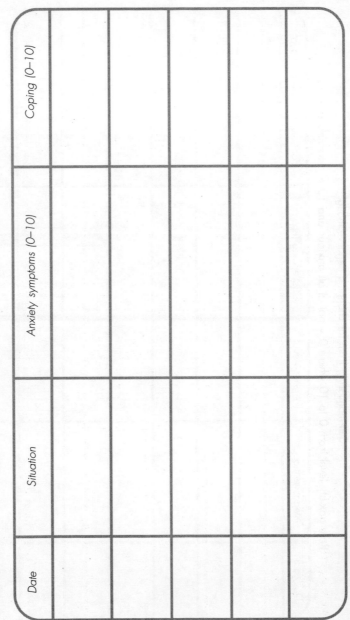

Date	Situation	Anxiety symptoms (0–10)	Coping (0–10)

Monitoring form for panic attacks

Date	Situation	Anxiety symptoms (0–10)	Coping (0–10)

Monitoring form for panic attacks

Date	Situation	Anxiety symptoms (0–10)	Coping (0–10)

Monitoring form for panic attacks

Date	Situation	Anxiety symptoms (0–10)	Coping (0–10)

Monitoring form for panic attacks

Date	Situation	Anxiety symptoms (0–10)	Coping (0–10)

Monitoring form for panic attacks

Date	Situation	Anxiety symptoms (0–10)	Coping (0–10)

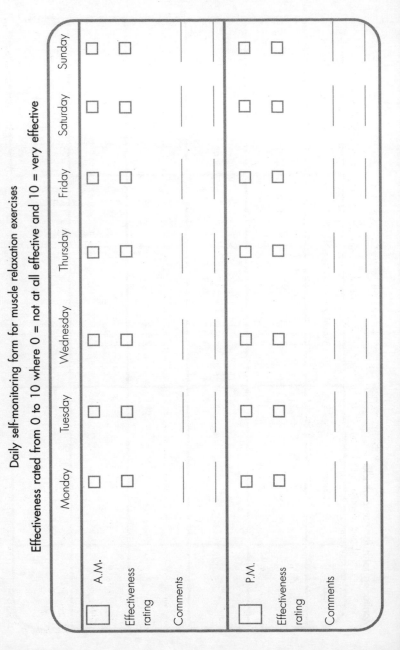

Daily self-monitoring form for muscle relaxation exercises

Effectiveness rated from 0 to 10 where 0 = not at all effective and 10 = very effective

	Monday	Tuesday	Wednesday	Thursday	Friday	Saturday	Sunday
A.M. ☐	☐	☐	☐	☐	☐	☐	☐
Effectiveness rating	☐	☐	☐	☐	☐	☐	☐
Comments							
P.M. ☐	☐	☐	☐	☐	☐	☐	☐
Effectiveness rating	☐	☐	☐	☐	☐	☐	☐
Comments							

Daily self-monitoring form for muscle relaxation exercises

Effectiveness rated from 0 to 10 where 0 = not at all effective and 10 = very effective

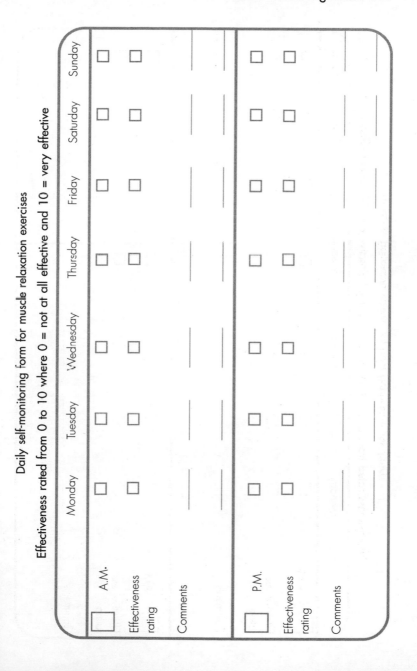

	Monday	Tuesday	Wednesday	Thursday	Friday	Saturday	Sunday
☐ A.M.	☐	☐	☐	☐	☐	☐	☐
Effectiveness rating	☐	☐	☐	☐	☐	☐	☐
Comments							
☐ P.M.	☐	☐	☐	☐	☐	☐	☐
Effectiveness rating	☐	☐	☐	☐	☐	☐	☐
Comments							

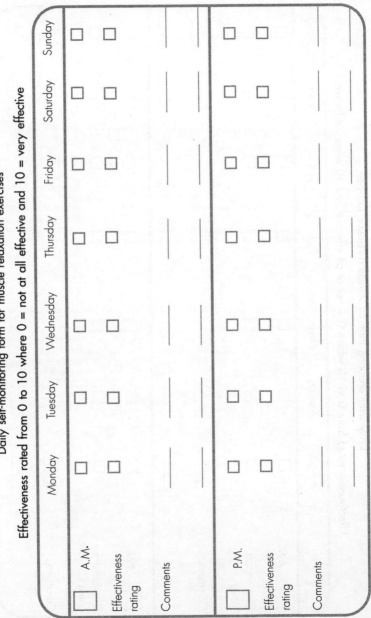

Daily self-monitoring form for muscle relaxation exercises

Effectiveness rated from 0 to 10 where 0 = not at all effective and 10 = very effective

	Monday	Tuesday	Wednesday	Thursday	Friday	Saturday	Sunday
A.M. ☐	☐	☐	☐	☐	☐	☐	☐
Effectiveness rating	☐	☐	☐	☐	☐	☐	☐
Comments							
P.M. ☐	☐	☐	☐	☐	☐	☐	☐
Effectiveness rating	☐	☐	☐	☐	☐	☐	☐
Comments							

Daily self-monitoring form for muscle relaxation exercises

Effectiveness rated from 0 to 10 where 0 = not at all effective and 10 = very effective

	Monday	Tuesday	Wednesday	Thursday	Friday	Saturday	Sunday
A.M. ☐	☐	☐	☐	☐	☐	☐	☐
Effectiveness rating	☐	☐	☐	☐	☐	☐	☐
Comments							
P.M. ☐	☐	☐	☐	☐	☐	☐	☐
Effectiveness rating	☐	☐	☐	☐	☐	☐	☐
Comments							

Daily self-monitoring form for muscle relaxation exercises

Effectiveness rated from 0 to 10 where 0 = not at all effective and 10 = very effective

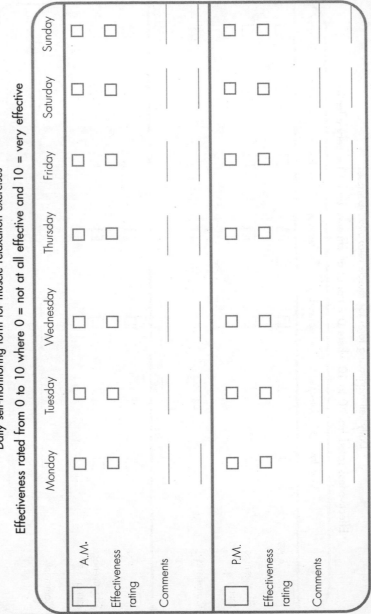

	Monday	Tuesday	Wednesday	Thursday	Friday	Saturday	Sunday
☐ A.M.	☐	☐	☐	☐	☐	☐	☐
	☐	☐	☐	☐	☐	☐	☐
Effectiveness rating							
Comments							
☐ P.M.	☐	☐	☐	☐	☐	☐	☐
	☐	☐	☐	☐	☐	☐	☐
Effectiveness rating							
Comments							

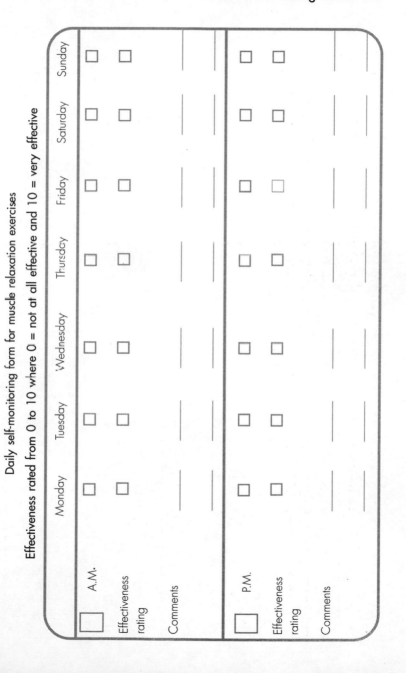

Daily self-monitoring form for muscle relaxation exercises

Effectiveness rated from 0 to 10 where 0 = not at all effective and 10 = very effective

	Monday	Tuesday	Wednesday	Thursday	Friday	Saturday	Sunday
A.M. ☐	☐	☐	☐	☐	☐	☐	☐
Effectiveness rating	☐	☐	☐	☐	☐	☐	☐
Comments							
P.M. ☐	☐	☐	☐	☐	☐	☐	☐
Effectiveness rating	☐	☐	☐	☐	☐	☐	☐
Comments							

Index